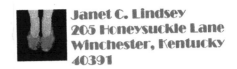
Creative Counseling Techniques:
An Illustrated Guide

Creative Counseling Techniques:
An Illustrated Guide

Ed Jacobs, Ph.D.

PAR **Psychological Assessment Resources, Inc.**
16204 N. Florida Avenue · Lutz, FL 33549 · 1.800.331.8378 · www.parinc.com

Illustrations: Ann Eblin
Cover Design: Mary Brunken

Published in 1992 by Psychological Assessment Resources, Inc., Odessa, FL 33556 USA

Library of Congress Cataloging-in-Publication Data
Jacobs, Edward E., 1944–
   Creative counseling techniques: an illustrated guide/ Ed Jacobs.
     p. cm.
   ISBN 0-911907-06-8 (pbk.)
   1. Counseling–Handbooks, manuals, etc.   I. Title.
   BF637.C6J33   1992
   158' .3--dc20   92-32487
                                          CIP

Published 1992.   5 6 7 8 9

Manufactured in the United States of America   Reorder #RO-2278

Acknowledgments

I have been writing this book in my head for over ten years, but it was only last year that I decided to write my ideas on paper. I wish to thank my many friends, former students, and former clients who encouraged me to write this book. I especially want to thank my two very close friends, Bob Masson and Karen Randolph, for their encouragement and support during the many stages of this book. Without their love and caring, I doubt if the book would have been completed.

The other set of people whom I want to acknowledge are the people associated with PAR (Psychological Assessment Resources, Inc.), my publisher. I wish to thank the president, Dr. Bob Smith, for believing in the book and deciding to publish it. I want to thank Serje Seminoff for his very warm and supportive help during the initial phases of the publishing process. I also want to thank Ann Eblin for the creative illustrations which make the text come alive. I especially want to thank my editors, Sandy Schneider and Jane Somers, for their tremendous effort and concern about the finished product. I could not have asked for two better people to work with. They were very professional, thorough, understanding, and dedicated. They made the project better and made the process enjoyable. I thank you!

Ed Jacobs
West Virginia University
Morgantown, West Virginia
August 1992

TABLE OF CONTENTS

PREFACE

Creative Counseling Techniques: An Illustrated Guide is a book for veteran therapists as well as for students or counselors new to the profession. It is a book that should be read over and over again since it is filled with brief explanations of many techniques and how they can be used. The first time you read this book, you will note certain techniques that you probably will use with clients in the near future. When you read the book again, other techniques will stand out. This is not a theoretical book; and in fact, it is assumed that the reader is either an experienced counselor with a strong understanding of theory or someone with at least a basic knowledge of theories and beginning counseling. Although some theories are mentioned, they are not discussed in any detail since this is a "how to" book.

The counseling approach described in this book is active, reflecting a belief that counseling is a dynamic, interactive, creative process. The emphasis is on skills and techniques that can be used to make counseling more concrete, engaging, and impactful.

The creative techniques and ideas presented here are useful to counselors in any setting. They can be used with all ages and in many different situations. Although most of the examples involve adult clients, therapists working with young children and teenagers will quickly see how the techniques are appropriate for these populations as well.

Organization

In the first chapter, I comment briefly on numerous aspects of counseling, such as advice giving, rapport, the use of theories, and taking the client deeper. The first chapter also includes an overview of creative counseling. In the next five chapters, I describe creative techniques: use of props, chairs, movement, writings and drawings, analogies, and fantasies. The last two chapters cover techniques that can be used in group counseling and in marriage and family counseling.

Language

Throughout the book, for convenience and brevity, I refer to the counselor and client as either "he" or "she" rather than the more awkward "he or she." The clients are men and women, boys and girls from various cultures. I use "counselor" and "therapist" interchangeably.

Comment

The techniques described in this book can be very helpful and impactful if they are used at the appropriate time and in the appropriate context. I do not attempt to teach timing and theoretical context in this book, but I want to emphasize their importance. Creative techniques can lead to very poor counseling if the therapist uses the techniques at the wrong time and/or in the wrong way. However, used correctly, the ideas presented in this book can greatly enhance your counseling!

1 Introduction

As I travel across the country conducting counseling workshops, I talk with hundreds of counselors in many different work settings. The vast majority of these counselors have been taught that counseling is a slow, "talking" process where the client does most of the talking while the counselor mostly listens. These counselors express tremendous frustration because they feel they need more skills and techniques. They have clients who want help and need help but don't seem to get better when the counselor uses common techniques and theories. With this dilemma in mind, I consider the following questions:

Does counseling *have to be* a slow process?

Is there a way to speed up the process?

Should the therapist be much more than a listener?

Is counseling only talking?

Are there some additional techniques that all counselors could use, regardless of their theoretical orientations?

I answer these important questions throughout this book.

What Is Counseling?

The first question that needs to be answered by all therapists is "What is counseling?" When I began studying counseling 25 years ago, I was introduced to the works of Sigmund Freud and Carl Rogers. I was taught that counseling was a process in which the client mostly talked to the counselor. I learned that the counselor's role was to provide a proper environment for the client to explore her feelings. Both Freud (1955) and Rogers (1951) believed that the therapist should take a fairly passive position in the counseling process, believing that the patient would gain much understanding of his problems if the counselor simply sat back and let him talk.

Later in my studying of therapy, I was exposed to the works of Albert Ellis and Fritz Perls. These two men took the position that the counselor could be very active and should challenge the client. Ellis's approach was primarily verbal, with the counselor disputing the irrational beliefs of the clients (Ellis, 1962). Perls (1969) was active in a different way by directing the client to do "chair work." That is, Perls had clients talking to parts of themselves or to another person by putting that "imagined" part or person in an empty chair. Both of these approaches were a refreshing change from Freud and Rogers because the pace of these approaches to counseling was much faster. As a result of my exposure to these approaches, I began to see that counseling can often move much quicker and that the counselor can be more active. I also began to see that counseling not only can be more than just talking, it often needs to be! More and more, I began to see counseling as a creative process where the counselor uses many different techniques in order to help her clients.

Unfortunately, counseling is often taught in such a way that counselors do not feel free to be very creative. When I conduct workshops on the topic of creative counseling, participants comment on feeling that they now have "permission" to be more active and imaginative. They say such things as, "Thanks for making counseling come alive; I knew I needed to do more than I was doing!" or "I appreciate your showing us how to make counseling more concrete and exciting!"

If you personally have felt your creativity stifled when counseling, this book should encourage you to be freer and more creative. Numerous examples are provided that illustrate the value of being creative. The book is filled with ideas and techniques that can be used in many different situations. The ideas presented are simple, yet most counselors have not thought of them or do not use them because no one ever encouraged counselors to do anything other than "talk." This book definitely encourage therapists to try different techniques.

A number of counselors use the term "creative counseling," and each has his or her own definition of what the term means. Gladding (1992) discusses the use of poetry, music, and art in therapy. Numerous authors write about play therapy and the use of puppets as a form of creative counseling with kids (Axline, 1969; Carter, 1987; James & Myer, 1987; Landreth, 1991). Nicholson and Golsan (1983) wrote that "creativity is set in motion through risk–the risk of moving beyond preset patterns of problem solving" (p. xi). In the best book that I have read on the subject of creative counseling, *Uncommon Therapy,* Haley (1986) describes many unique and creative techniques used by the late Milton Erickson, who had the courage to use unconventional counseling techniques. In many ways, this book also is about being unconventional; and it is about COURAGE. In fact, a sub-title for this book could be "The Courage to Counsel."

In this book, the term "creative counseling" refers to using techniques other than just talking in order to have impact on the client and/or the counseling process. I present the use of five different visual and experiential techniques: props; chairs; movement; drawings, lists, and diagrams; and analogies and fantasies. Although the book's emphasis is on individual counseling, there are also chapters on group counseling and marriage and family counseling.

Why Creative Techniques?

The reasons for using creative techniques are summarized very well by Young (1992): "At some point in every therapist's academic training, a great thirst for practical methods develops... This urge often comes when our favorite theoretical system appears to become inadequate" (p. 1). Counselors "in the trenches" have found that they need many different ways to approach their clients. Counseling is more than just theory and is now seen by many as strategy. Okun (1992) said, "The successful helper is familiar with many approaches and strategies" (p.7). Haley (1986) stated, "Therapy can be called strategic if the clinician initiates what happens during therapy and designs a particular approach for each problem" (p. 17). Nickerson and O'Laughlin (1982) pointed out that using only "talking" in counseling limits our potential as helpers.

Counseling can and should be a very creative activity, allowing you to be more effective as a counselor. Gladding (1992) stated: "Effective counselors are aware of the multidimensional qualities of the counseling process and utilize them effectively in the uniqueness that is their own style" (p. ix). My intent in this book is to encourage counselors to be active and innovative when the opportunity arises. Throughout the years, I have heard a number of counselors complain about being burned-out or bored. The creative techniques discussed in this book will most likely prevent boredom, because the counseling process will become more interesting and engaging. The techniques presented will also provide you with a number of different ways to address the various problems in counseling. Using creative techniques also adds variety to counseling and helps to prevent burn-out. Below are seven additional reasons for using creative techniques. Included are some brief examples.

1. To make concepts more concrete

People with problems are often confused and do not understand why their lives are going awry. When these people seek counseling, they often do not get a clear picture of their specific problems–thus the counseling experience is vague and confusing. Egan (1990) pointed out that counseling needs to be clear and specific in order to move the process forward. The creative techniques described in this book allow the counselor to make the counseling more clear and concrete. For instance, the chapter on props discusses using a styrofoam cup with holes in it as a way to help the client see the "holes" in his self-esteem. The chapter on the use of chairs describes the client sitting in a small child's chair to experience how he is being a little boy.

2. To heighten awareness

Clients often are unaware of their behavior. Helping clients become more aware is one goal of therapy. Perls (1969) said that "awareness is curative." Creative techniques can help make clients more aware of what they are doing. For example, in the chapter on creative movement, a simple technique is described where the therapist stands on a chair to heighten the client's awareness of just how much he is looking up to his father. In the chapter on props, a rubber band is used to heighten the client's awareness of the tension she is feeling.

3. To dramatize a point

Creative techniques can be used to dramatize a point (Gladding, 1992). For instance, a client may be totally focused on his wife who has left him. For weeks all he does is think about his wife; and when he comes for counseling, he says the same thing about her week after week. By having him stand in the corner, facing inward, the counselor allows the client to experience his narrow thinking and to see what he is doing to himself. This technique and similar ones are described in the chapter on the use of movement as a creative technique. Having a client hold heavy weights also dramatizes what she is doing.

4. To speed up the counseling process

By using some creative techniques, the counseling process can sometimes be quickened. Egan (1990) discussed how the counselor should develop a bias toward action in order to move counseling along. For instance, if the client is going on and on about her indecision to stay married or get divorced, the counselor may simply put two chairs a few feet apart in front of her and ask her "to sit in both chairs at the same time." This will usually cause the client to stop and think. By having the visual image in front of her, the decision she faces becomes more concrete, and she may realize more quickly what she is doing.

5. To enhance learning, because people are visual learners

The example above is one of visual learning. Another visual technique is the use of drawings. Clients seeing how they are enmeshed can be very helpful. For example, if a mother is too emotionally involved with her son, the counselor could draw the following:

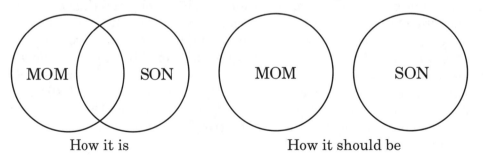

How it is   How it should be

6. To enhance learning, because people learn through experience

Clients often learn more by doing something rather than by talking about it. The client who says he wants to change, but does nothing to change, may benefit from being asked to hold onto the chair he is sitting in while trying to move to the chair across the room. This experience usually generates insight and discussion. As Zinker (1977) said, "The therapist helps the client to be the experimenter, the teacher, the active modifier..." (p. 22).

7. To focus the session

Creative techniques are also very useful in focusing the session. Too often, either the client or the counselor causes the session to lose its focus. Creative techniques can be used as points of reference, thus helping greatly to keep the session on track. The chart mentioned in the next section can improve the counselor's awareness of the focus and its depth.

Counseling and the Counseling Process

Although the purpose of this book is to acquaint you with different creative techniques, I thought that it also would be appropriate and helpful to share briefly some general thoughts about counseling and the counseling process that I have come to believe during my 20 years as a counselor educator.

Focusing: Getting, Holding, Shifting, and Deepening the Focus

The counseling process can be viewed as a "focusing" process. The process is one of getting, holding, shifting, and deepening the focus. That is, the counselor first listens, then gets the client focused on a relevant issue. The counselor should be aware of the need to either hold or shift the focus. If it does shift, she must then decide either to stay with the new topic or go back to the original focus.

Many counselors don't realize that effective counseling really is about focusing. In order to have impact, the therapist needs to make sure that the focus is held long enough and taken deep enough for growth, learning, or insight (Jacobs, Harvill, & Masson, 1988).

The 10-1 Depth Chart

One way to think of a counseling session is in terms of the focus moving down and up a 10-1 scale with 10 representing a new topic or the surface of an issue and 1 representing deep involvement in the issue. By using the analogy of a depth chart you can get a picture of the flow of your counseling sessions. For instance, let's say that Carrie came to counseling and brought up four topics. She first talked about the problems she was having with her youngest son; then she talked about her teenage daughter. Next she discussed her need to control everything, and then she brought up the trouble she was having with her in-laws. Let's also assume that she did not stay focused on any of the subjects very long. Using the depth chart analogy, the session would be charted something like this:

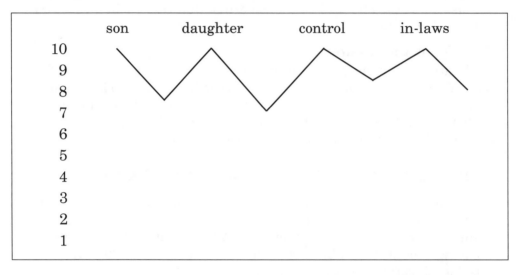

Before reading on, you may want to consider the flow and depth of your sessions. Are you holding the focus long enough so that the client can gain some insight into her issue? Are your sessions going below an 8? They should.

The use of some prop, movement, or written activity can often focus the session so that a depth greater than 8 can be achieved. Very little impact occurs in counseling unless the focus is held long enough for the client to gain some new insight. By having the client see a drawing of "enmeshment" or hold a cassette tape representing the tapes in her head, the counselor can focus the client on what she is doing to herself and what she needs to do differently. The use of such techniques takes the focus to a depth of 7 or below and often makes the counseling more concrete and helpful.

The Use of Theory

The skilled therapist is always aware of the flow of counseling and tries to focus the session by using one of the many counseling theories. For the purpose of this book, counseling theories are briefly discussed as they relate to the use of creative techniques. It is my strong belief that all counseling should have a theoretical base and that the use of any technique mentioned in this book needs to be integrated into your theoretical approach(es) to counseling. If you do not feel well grounded in theory, I would suggest you find one or two theories that you like and attend workshops on the them. Also, do as much reading as possible on your chosen theories. **Theory is a must!** Do not be a "cop-out eclectic" counselor! A "cop-out eclectic" is one who knows a little about many theories. A true eclectic counselor is a person who knows a lot about a number of theories and pulls from many of them during counseling (Corey, 1991; Corsini & Wedding, 1989; Meier, 1989).

Rapport

Good rapport with the client is very important (Carkhuff, 1987; Egan, 1990; Okun, 1992). A skilled counselor always monitors how the counseling relationship is developing. Unfortunately, rapport building is sometimes taught incorrectly or is misunderstood by the beginning counselor. Many people have been taught that the first session or two should be devoted to rapport. This simply is not true. With some clients, the rapport is instantaneous or automatic (Dinkmeyer, Dinkmeyer, & Sperry, 1987). That is, the client in a crisis is in such need of help that he pays little or no attention to the counselor except in wanting her to help him. Thus, the counselor can begin helping within the first 3 or 4 minutes of the session (Gilliland & James, 1988). There are many times when it takes one or two sessions for rapport to be established, but it is best not to establish a rule that the entire first session must be devoted to rapport building.

Students frequently ask me, "How fast should you move in counseling?" I tell them to move as quickly as possible, but to keep in mind that **the most important thing is timing.** I relate timing to shifting a car—one can shift too early or too late. Some clients are ready to work as soon as they sit down, and others are slow to warm up. Effective timing requires the counselor to pay very close attention to the needs of the client in the opening few minutes of a session, especially in the first session.

Ways Counselors Can Be Harmful

In very simple terms, there are three ways that counselors can be harmful to clients. The first is by giving poor advice, wrongly interpreting some information, or saying something incorrect due to lack of knowledge, unfinished business, or personal values (Meier, 1989). The second way that clients may be harmed is when the counselor acts unethically, such as breaking confidentiality or making inappropriate sexual advances toward a client (Corey, 1991).

The third way that a therapist can be harmful is by moving so slowly that the client feels that nothing happens in counseling, so she quits coming, believing that counseling cannot be helpful to her. Many times I have had clients tell me that they have gone to counseling before, but it was not helpful because the counselor "did nothing–just sat there and listened!"

Boxing Analogy

Counseling takes on many different forms because there are so many different problems with which to deal. Sometimes counseling is a very supportive process, while other times it is an educational process. There are still other times when counseling is a consultative/ informational process, and times when counseling is a therapeutic process that may cause the client to look at some painful aspects of his life. The most difficult for counselors is therapeutic counseling.

I use boxing as an analogy to describe the therapeutic process. Many beginning counselors only throw jabs in the session, and the client doesn't change. Some counselors realize that they need more than jabs, so they develop some combination punches. However, when the client says "ouch," the counselor backs off, almost as if to say, "Oops, I'm sorry." The truth of the matter is the counselor needs a strategy that includes jabs, combination punches, knock out punches, and the determination not to back off when he gets the client on the "ropes." It is important that the counselor realize that **People Don't Change Easily.** He needs to be sensitive to the client and, when it is appropriate, do whatever it takes to help the client get through his impasse (Cormier & Cormier, 1985; Egan, 1990; Perls, 1969).

Cutting Off

To be an effective counselor, you have to be willing to cut off and refocus the client. If the counselor is afraid to interrupt the client, she will not be able to control the focus in many instances because many clients will ramble on and on (Egan, 1990; Ellis & Dryden, 1987). To cut off, I say something like this:

> "I understand what you are getting at. Now what do you want to do about it?"

OR

> "I understand that he is horrible, but it really doesn't help me to hear more stories about him. I think we need to look at how all of this is affecting you today."

OR

> "Hold on, Juan, let's stay with one topic at a time. Let's finish with your mom before we go to the business with your brother."

There are many instances when you would not want to interrupt the client, but I am including this section in case you feel you need "permission" to redirect your clients.

Asking Questions

In most counseling programs, one of the first things students are taught is not to ask many questions because they need to understand that counseling is a process and that questions tend to detract from building a therapeutic relationship (Meier, 1989). In the real world of counseling, however, asking questions is not only okay, it is necessary. The skilled counselor learns how to ask questions and build the relationship at the same time (Egan, 1990; Wubbolding, 1986). The therapist who chooses to ask a number of questions needs to use his voice to show that he wants to be helpful and truly cares. It is not wrong to ask questions unless the counselor pays no attention to the relationship and sounds like an uninvolved doctor or detective.

The Use of Your Voice

One of the most important tools to have in your "counseling tool box" is your voice. Many counselors use only one or two different voice patterns regardless of the problem being dealt with. There are times when your voice should be slow, deliberate, and supportive, while other times using a "cognitive" voice, which is a more "factual" rather than supportive voice, would be more appropriate. Most of the time, your voice pattern should match that of your client's, but there will be times when you should intentionally use your voice to try to alter his mood. Remember, **good counseling requires good use of your voice!**

Listening to the Client's Voice

By listening to your client's voice, you can usually tell his state of mind (in TA terms, which ego state he is in). Often the voice can give you some ideas of how the client is feeling and how he is operating in the world (Egan, 1990; Okun, 1992). A very rapid voice usually means the client is not thinking, but rather is anxious or is simply playing some "tape" in his head. A very slow, deliberate voice may mean that he has a strong need to be exact and perfect. A soft, scared voice usually means the client is in his Child ego state. Voice patterns can provide a wealth of information and understanding for the counselor who listens. **It is essential for the counselor to be aware of speech patterns, because so much understanding can come from carefully listening to the client's voice.**

Advice

All counseling programs and most beginning counseling textbooks emphasize that counselors should not give advice (Cavanagh, 1990; Meier, 1989). I believe there are many times when it is not only appropriate to give advice, but it would almost be unethical not to. For instance, if a client is in a rage and is going to confront his boss in an out-of-control manner, a good counselor would advise the client not to do so. The point of this example is that giving advice often makes sense, and the advice given is very helpful for the client. Certainly you need to be careful with any advice, making sure that your own values are not getting in the way. The rule of "Never give advice" is not a good one. Once you are out in the work world, I would suggest you adopt a position regarding advice that works best for you and your clients.

Touching

Most counselors have come to realize that proper touching of clients can be therapeutic when used appropriately (Mintz, 1982; Willison & Masson, 1986). By touching, I mean using simple gestures, such as laying your hand on the client's shoulder or taking the client's hand when he is crying. Unfortunately, there are some counselors who have touched their clients inappropriately. Consequently, some training programs now teach "never touch your client." I teach that it is okay to touch your client as long as you only do it to benefit the client and always monitor the reaction to your touch. Certain clients do not want to be touched, while others may try to manipulate you into touching them.

When used appropriately, therapeutic touch can be a helpful technique. As I write this, I think, "Well, shouldn't it just be something spontaneous and not a technique?" The answer is "yes and no." Touching certainly should be genuine; at the same time, a good counselor rarely does or says anything without first considering the impact. Experience with your clients helps you to develop the ability to know if touching is appropriate and therapeutic.

Giving the Client a Recording of the Session

Often, I tape record the session and then give the tape to the client. Many clients have said that listening to the tape was as beneficial as the session because they had time to really process what happened. Some have reported listening to the tape as many as five or six times.

Length and Frequency of Sessions

There is no magic to the 50-minute hour. In schools, clients are usually seen for less time. In my private practice, sessions usually are between 50 and 65 minutes, but they are sometimes longer or shorter, depending on the nature of the problem. The frequency standard is to see the client once a week, but this really depends on the situation. There are times when I see the client every day or every other day, and then there are clients that I only see every 2 weeks. Instead of locking yourself into rigid thinking about how counseling should be, do what it takes rather than follow some set of rules.

Homework

The idea of asking the client to perform different tasks between sessions makes good sense. Homework can be anything: reading, writing or an assigned activity. Walen, DiGiuseppe, and Wessler (1980) devote an entire chapter to homework as it relates to the counseling process. Counseling once a week with no reading or other tasks to do between sessions will often lead to the same results as a person who takes piano lessons once a week but does not practice in between—the person rarely improves. Egan (1990) commented that "the real work of helping is what the client does 'out there'" (p. 180).

Recovering addicts work a recovery program. A person in recovery may read something daily, attend AA meetings, and work on 1 of the 12 steps. I think counselors can learn from this model in that, no matter what approach to counseling we use, we should have clients do homework or work a program that involves completing various tasks outside of the session. Throughout this book, I make reference to homework assignments, which can be anything that facilitates the client's growth and/or awareness.

Sponsor Model

For the last 10 years, I have been studying addictions and recovery. There are a number of aspects of AA from which the counseling field could learn. One aspect I am particularly impressed with is the emphasis placed on the value of a newly recovering person finding a sponsor with whom he can talk regularly (Rogers & McMillin, 1989). Often the sponsor asks the recovering person to call daily, even though they may only talk 5 to 10 minutes. This seems to be very valuable for a person just starting recovery. Counselors, on the other hand, usually see the client only once a week and tell the client not to call unless it is an absolute emergency. Many counselor educators and supervisors worry about dependency developing, but for many clients the contact would be extremely helpful and reassuring. I think we need to give more thought to our interaction pattern with clients and be flexible enough to come up with a pattern that is most beneficial for the client.

Essentials for Counseling

Before moving to the next chapter, I want to briefly comment on what I see as essential items for a counselor's office, other than the necessary two chairs. These essentials include the following items:

1. **A wipe board and/or a large pad**

   This is extremely useful in writing out goals, lists, TA ego states, and other drawings and charts that will be discussed in Chapter 5.

2. **A small chair**

   Even if you don't use TA as one of your theoretical models, reference to the little boy or girl in clients comes up often in counseling. Certainly the current work in co-dependency and the wounded child can be enhanced by having a small child's chair to refer to.

3. **Two extra chairs**

   Often in counseling, clients will be working on issues that relate to another person, or they will talk about the splits within themselves regarding a particular issue. By having empty chairs to represent the other person or their splits, the client can get a better sense of what is happening. Creative techniques with chairs are covered in more depth in Chapter 3.

4. **Various props: cups, tapes, shields**

   Many counseling concerns deal with self-esteem. One excellent way to symbolize "holes in one's self-esteem" is through the use of styrofoam or paper cups. Another prop, cassette tapes, can be used to make the concept of the different rules, messages, or "tapes" in the client's head more concrete. When a client talks about communication problems with his parents, spouse, or boss, a shield can be used to show him what he may need to do when talking with that person. Use of props in counseling is the focus of Chapter 2.

2 Use of Props in Counseling

In this chapter, I describe numerous props that can be used in counseling to help focus the client, heighten the client's awareness of her issue, and/or help the client get a better sense of what she is doing to herself. Any prop described is used as an aid to the counselor and should be used in conjunction with basic counseling skills such as listening carefully to the client and coming from the client's frame of reference. In discussing the props, different kinds of problems will be referred to as well as several theories. It is beyond the scope of this book to delve deeply into any specific problem or theory. It is assumed that the reader has already learned or is still learning about the different theories and ways to approach various problems.

Throughout the chapter, I give many examples of counseling scenarios. In the examples, I begin the dialogue where the counselor is introducing the prop. I ask you to imagine the dialogue that has preceded the counselor's introduction. I also end the scenarios when I feel that I have given enough dialogue for you to see the value of the creative technique. In other words, I am mainly focusing on the use of the technique and not on how to solve the problem presented. I feel that if I can give a few examples, you will be able to come up with many other variations using the same prop.

Cups

1. Holes in self-esteem

Clients very often feel that they have low self-esteem due to what has happened to them in the past or due to comments that people have made (Bradshaw, 1988; Branden, 1987).

Counselor: I want you to take this cup and think of it as your self-esteem. From what you have been saying, you have a number of holes in your self-esteem. Now, with this pencil *(pen, scissors)* I want you to punch holes of various sizes to represent the holes in your self-esteem... *(Client punches a number of holes.)* What do you see?

Client: I've got lots of holes, especially a big one from my dad... What do I do about all the holes?

13

Counselor: That really is the point of counseling. We have to figure out how you can plug the leaks–otherwise, you are bound to feel bad. Which hole do you want to work on first?

I have had clients take their cups home with them and put them in places where they can be seen everyday so as to remind them about trying to plug their leaks.

To dramatize the effects of the holes, you can pour water into the cup; and the client will obviously see it run out. This demonstration may be useful if the client cannot accept compliments or positive strokes.

You can also take two cups, the one with holes and one that has no holes, and put them on two different chairs in front of the client and have the client talk about how the two cups are different.

Counselor: What would be the difference in a person in this chair with all the holes and a person in the other chair *(cup with no holes)*?

Client: The person with no holes is going to feel much better about himself.

2. Love addiction

A cup with a hole in it can be used to help people who feel they desperately need love (Forward, 1986; Halpern, 1982; Norwood, 1985).

Counselor: Take this cup and punch a hole in the bottom. *(Client punches a hole.)* If this represents your "love cup" and you need to keep it filled, what happens if people pour into it.

Client:	You mean if someone poured anything into this cup, it would leak out quickly because of the hole in the bottom.
Counselor:	That's right. And when people do pour into you, you feel good for a short while and then, due to your leak, you feel empty.
Client:	Well, what do I do to stay full?
Counselor:	You have a couple of choices. You can desperately run around getting all kinds of people to love you so that someone is always pouring into the cup, or you can plug up the leak and try to love yourself more.
Client:	I guess what you are saying is that the reason I always have two or three lovers is because of the hole in my cup. Boy, this cup thing sure makes it clear to me. I don't want this.

3. Personal worth

A cup can represent the client's worth that she puts in someone else's hand, usually a lover, but can be parents, boss, children (Ellis & Harper, 1975). In the example below, the client has been talking about how her boyfriend makes her "feel so worthless."

Counselor:	I want you to assume that this cup is your personal worth. Take it in your hand. I'm going to be your boyfriend for a minute. *(The counselor then stands in front of her and reaches for the cup.)* When you met your boyfriend you handed over your worth to him. *(The counselor takes the cup and stands on a chair in front of the client.)* Now he has your worth in his hand, and he periodically smashes it. *(The counselor, who is playing her boyfriend, squeezes the cup.)*
Client:	*(Looking up at the counselor on the chair)* You really have it pinpointed! How do I change this?

The counselor now has the client very aware of what she is doing to herself, and he can help her work through this by staying with the concept of getting her worth back into her own hands. The counselor can give the cup to the client and have her hold onto it as the counselor *(playing the boyfriend)* tries to get it away from her.

Playdough

Playdough is a useful prop because it can be torn apart and then put back together, which in a sense is often what is going on in counseling. Playdough can be used to symbolize the client and how he has several parts that are bothering him.

Example 1

Counselor: I want you to work this playdough into a solid ball... Okay, now I want to show you what is happening in counseling. Each week you come in and talk about something that is bothering you. Let's see, you talked about Dad *(counselor takes a chunk of the playdough and puts the chunk in a seat across from the client while the client holds the larger piece in his hand)*. You talked about your marriage *(counselor takes another chunk and places it in the seat)*; you also talked about your being overweight and about your job *(counselor takes two more chunks and places them in the chair, leaving the client with just a small piece in his hand)*. What do you see?

Client: Most of me is over there in the chair.

Counselor: That is one way to look at it. What I see is that each week you add a piece to the chair rather than reversing the process. We need to focus on the things in the chair and try to resolve them so that the chunk in your hand can start to get larger. You will begin to feel better when you start working on your issues. Let's pick one and focus on that one for today.

Client: Okay. My marriage.

Counselor: Now our goal is to work today and maybe even the next few sessions on your marriage with the idea that we have to start getting pieces from the chair back into your hands.

Client: Right. This helps me to see what I have been doing and what I need to do.

Counselor: Good. What about your marriage do you need to clear up?

Example 2

Counselor: Take this piece of playdough and tell me how it feels.

Client: *(Client handles playdough for a minute or so.)* It feels firm, solid.

Counselor: Now split it in half and put one piece over in the chair. Now, how does it feel?

Client: Not as big. Not as strong.

Counselor: Isn't this what you are doing? You seem to me to have yourself split between the two, and it is no wonder you are feeling less confident.

Client: The difference in how the playdough feels with only half of it sure makes the point. I cannot keep splitting myself off. It doesn't feel good at all!

Cassette Tapes

Many client issues result from what clients believe about themselves. Numerous theories address this notion. The rational-emotive therapist talks about irrational ideas (Ellis & Dryden, 1987). The transactional analysis counselor talks about Parent tapes and Child tapes (Berne, 1972). The Adlerians use terms such as mistaken goals, guiding fictions, and private logic (Dreikurs, 1953). Regardless of the orientation to counseling, most therapists will, at times, discuss with their clients some of the clients' mistaken ideas or "shoulds." To help the client get a more visual picture of this idea, cassette tapes can be used.

1. Replacing the tapes

Counselor: Here's what I'm seeing. *(Counselor holds a tape up in his hand.)* You have this tape in your head that plays constantly saying, "I'm no good." *(Counselor writes on the tape "no good" and gives it to the client.)* You play it at various volumes, turning it up to volume 10 in situations with your girlfriend and when you interact with Mom.

Client: But I am no good.

Counselor: No, you feel that you are no good, and you tell yourself that. You were taught to tell yourself that. What I want to do is get you to make a different tape that is the truth about you. *(Counselor hands the client another tape with the word "truth" on it.)*

From a theoretical point of view, the counselor would be set up for disputing the client's irrational self-talk using either RET or for helping him edit his "not okay Child tapes" using TA.

2. Editing the tapes

Another way to use cassette tapes is to talk about the client needing to edit some of the "tapes" in her head. The counselor can give the client an old cassette tape and have her tell about things that need editing. As she talks about them, the counselor asks her to begin editing the tape by pulling out a piece of tape and then cutting it off so that she ends up with a pile of edited tape lying at her feet. This gives the client a mental image of what she needs to do in counseling. (See illustration on next page.)

3. Erasing the tapes

A variation of editing the tape can be done by actually recording the "negative self-talk." The counselor would then have the client listen to what she is saying to herself and get her to realize that the self-talk needs to be changed. He would work with her to come up with more rational, self-affirming self-talk. The counselor would then have the client remake the tape, recording over the first tape, thus erasing it.

Counselor: *(After just erasing the old tape)* Now let's listen to the tape and hear those negative things.

Client: But we can't. We just erased them.

Counselor: True. *(Silence for a minute or so.)*

Client: That's great!! I see what you are getting at.

This technique very clearly points out what the client is doing to herself and how she needs to erase the things that she is telling herself.

Playing Cards

Many clients don't believe that they can change; and no matter how much you encourage them, they just hold onto their old habits (Egan, 1990; Nugent, 1990; Shulman, 1984). When discussion of the need for changing doesn't seem to work, I have tried the following creative technique. I ask the client if he knows how to play poker. If he says yes, I take out a deck of cards and start to deal for Five Card Draw.

Counselor: Okay, I'm going to take ___ cards *(depending on the hand dealt)*.

Client: What about me? I want ___ cards.

Counselor: No, you just have to play the hand you were dealt.

I repeat this for numerous hands showing the client that, by playing more than just the hand I was dealt, I am able to win much more than he is. This invariably leads to a pointed discussion about change, and I keep referring to the cards and saying that he can ask for cards and better his hand! This often helps the client to get the point about change.

Post-It Pads

Often the insights that clients gain during a session do not "stick" with them once they leave the counselor's office. A client can say to the counselor that he feels okay about himself, but then he reports that all week he was really critical of himself.

In the example below, the counselor has been talking with Tom for a number of sessions. Tom has just been describing how bad he felt the day before during recess. The little boy feels bad about himself because he is not good at sports, and other kids make fun of him. The counselor has been trying to get Tom to see that he is okay even if he is not athletic. The boy seems to understand, but when he leaves and has to face other kids, he forgets what he has worked on in the session.

Counselor: Tom, we have to do something else in the session. It's like this. On this card I've got written "I'm okay." I want you to put this card on your chest. This is like what we do in here. You tell me you are okay even if the kids call you names. Now take your hand away from the card and watch what happens. What do you see?

Client: It doesn't stay. It falls off.

Counselor: Right. What we do here is not sticking. We have to get what we say here to stick! Now take this Post-It and write on it what you believe about yourself, then stick it on your chest... See, it is sticking. What can we do to get this to happen?

This example highlights the problem of counseling not having the impact that it needs to help this boy. The counselor can use this prop to keep asking the boy if it is "sticking."

Band-Aid Box

For counselors who have clients who don't want to work on important issues but need to, a Band-Aid box can be used to emphasize the difference between productive counseling and mere "Band-Aid" counseling.

Counselor: I have here a box filled with Band-Aids. Maria, I think you need to decide if you want counseling or if you want a Band-Aid that will wash off in a few days.

This can lead to a productive discussion about how the client is approaching counseling.

Shield

Often in counseling the presenting problem deals with communication and how a person feels attacked by her parent, boss, spouse, or some other significant person. Many counselors talk to clients about protecting themselves but do not really demonstrate the process. By using a shield, the counselor can give the client a visual, experiential memory, thus enhancing the counseling. This is especially true for teenagers when they are discussing problems they are having with their parents. It also can be helpful to young kids who are having trouble at home or at school. Another large population who feel attacked and can benefit from the use of the shield are those who live with an alcoholic or a rageaholic.

One approach to the problem is to teach the client to deflect the hurtful comments. A shield can be used to dramatize the effects of protecting or not protecting oneself from the attacks. (I use an 8 inch by 11 inch plexiglass shield.)

Counselor: Let me show you something. Take this shield in your hands; and as I try to poke you, raise the shield to protect yourself... Okay. Now as I try to poke you, don't use the shield *(counselor pokes client in the chest)*. If you don't learn to use the shield, you'll feel hurt. I want to teach you how to shield yourself and how to stay in your Adult ego state (from Transactional Analysis) when you are around those people.

In this case, the counselor would help the client understand if he does not shield himself, he will more than likely continue to feel very hurt around his girlfriend, dad, and grandmother. [Note: Male counselors should not poke female clients in the chest, but might, instead, aim the poke at a female's shoulder to make the same point.]

In this next example, the counselor refers specifically to the client's alcoholic father.

Client: It hurts so bad when he yells at me and calls me stupid and no good.

Counselor: Is this usually when he is drinking?

Client: Yes, but he shouldn't do it!

Counselor: Melvin, I need to teach you many things about alcoholism. First, let me teach you something that you need to do when your dad is drinking. I am going to stand here and play your dad. I'll demonstrate his messages by poking you in the chest. You're stupid *(pokes his chest)*. You're lazy *(pokes him)*. You're no good *(pokes him)*.

Client: That's how it feels.

Counselor: Here, take this shield. *(The counselor hands him a large plexiglass shield.)* Now as I say these things, use the shield to keep them from getting to your chest. *(The client holds the shield and blocks the counselor's hand as the counselor says nasty things to him.)*

Client: This feels better. How do I learn to do this? I don't like it, but it is better.

Counselor: True. I wish you didn't have to shield yourself, but the fact is, you do.

Many times clients have come back the following week and said something like, "I had to use my shield three times this week and it worked!"

Filter

In family, marital, and work situations, communication problems arise. There will be times when the counselor will talk with the client about not taking things so personally and about how she may need to filter some of the comments. Below is the dialogue from a session with a teenager and her family. The discussion was about the problem the girl had with her stepfather's negative comments.

Counselor: Let me show you something. Do you know what this is? *(Counselor hands girl a furnace filter.)*

Client: It's a filter of some sort.

Counselor: Do you know what filters are for?

Client: Uh, I don't know. Uh, to filter the crap out of the air.

Counselor: Yes, that's right! To filter the crap and let the good things through.

The counselor then would talk about how she could learn to filter the "crap" from her stepfather.

Walls

Often clients will talk about the walls they have built up. Some walls are between them and other people, and other times the walls are between them and the world. To dramatize this, the counselor can ask the client to hold up his wall. (The wall can be the plexiglass shield mentioned above, a briefcase, or any other appropriate object.)

1. The fear of getting close

Counselor: Brent, let me show you what you are doing. I am going to play your friend who you want to get close to. Let's stand up. *(The counselor and client stand a couple of feet apart.)* I want you to take this briefcase and, using both hands, hold it up to represent your wall. *(Client is now holding the briefcase in his hands.)* Now, as your friend, I am reaching out, and I want you to embrace me while still holding onto your wall.

Client:	I can't embrace you unless I let go of the briefcase... Oh, unless I let go of my wall. Boy, this is right on. Those walls have been there a long time.

Counselor: I know. I am going to remove the wall slowly, just to give you a sense of how that would feel. *(The counselor slowly takes the wall from the client, and then the two are standing without the wall.)*

Client: I like this better even though it feels scary.

Counselor: I know it is scary. Let's do two things. Let's look at when and why you built those walls, and let's look at your self-talk; that is, how you are scaring yourself by what you are telling yourself.

2. Isolation

Counselor: It's like you have built up this wall, and now you are back behind it. I want you to move over to this seat, and I am going to put this partition in front of you. *(The client moves, and the counselor places a large, movable partition in front of the client.)*

Client: *(In a sad voice)* This is how it feels.

Counselor: What we have to do is get you to want to get out from behind there. Is life very interesting back there?

Client: Heck no!

Counselor: By the end of today, we at least should be able to get you to look around from the wall, and then we'll keep working until you are out from behind there.

Client: Can I go back to my regular seat now?

Counselor: *(In a kind voice)* No, I think we should do the session with you back there unless you are ready to be done with your wall.

Client: No, not yet. But this experience is helping me to see how I'm limiting myself.

Beer Bottle

Counselors often will be faced with clients who drink or who have a family member who drinks.

1. Short fuse

A beer bottle and a piece of string can be helpful in showing what happens when a person drinks.

Counselor: Let me use this bottle and string to demonstrate something. You have a reasonably long fuse when you are not drinking. *(Counselor holds up string that is about 6 to 8 inches long.)* Now look what happens to your fuse when you drink. *(Counselor slowly eases the string into the bottle until it disappears.)*

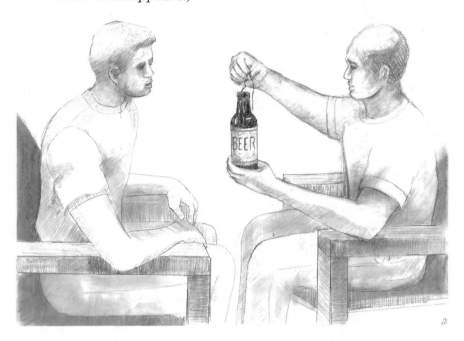

By graphically showing the client what happens to him or his loved one who drinks, the counselor can drive home the point that as long as the person drinks, there will be problems.

2. Poor contact with loved one

Client: I can't stand the way he is. We used to get along great, but now it's really getting bad. I need more from him. I want it to be like it was. I don't understand.

Counselor: Let me get you to do something. Hold up your two hands. One hand represents you, and the other represents your husband. I want you to clasp your hands together. This is how it used to be.

Client: Yes! We were close—real close.

Counselor: Okay, now I want you to take this beer bottle and clasp your hands together.

Client: I can't.

Counselor: Squeeze the bottle and see if you can do it.

Client: There's no way unless the bottle is gone.

Counselor: You've got it. I don't think you can be close to him as long as he continues to drink. You've got to quit denying that fact. I hope this demonstration helps.

Client: It most definitely does. Boy, this sure makes it clear.

Both of these examples are useful in showing the effects of alcohol and may help in overcoming the resistance that the alcoholic and her family often exhibit.

If you are counseling many alcoholics, an excellent prop would be one of those large (5-foot) balloon-like cans of beer. There are many creative ways in which it could be used.

Rubber Band

1. Tension

Clients often complain about being stretched to the limit. A rubber band can be used to symbolize this tension.

Counselor: Take this rubber band and stretch it. Stretch it to its limit. Now a little more.

Client: Wow! This is how it feels.

Counselor: We have got to get you to reduce the tension. Pick one area of your life that you are willing to change, and let's work on it.

Often families are stretched by their defiant teenager.

Client: I can't stand the way she is acting. I won't put up with it. Right now she's grounded for the rest of the year, and we have the door off her room so that we can see her! I don't know why she's being so hateful.

Counselor: Are things getting better or worse?

Client: Worse!

Counselor: Here's what I am worried about. Take this rubber band and stretch it to very close to its limit. *(Client does this and winces as she stares at it.)* I am afraid that the situation is very close to the breaking point.

Client: Oh, it is!

Counselor: I need to get you to see that if you keep doing what you are doing, it'll break. Stretch the rubber band just a little bit more. *(Client does this.)* What can we do to ease this situation. You keep wanting her to do something, and evidently she's not going to. I don't think you want her to run away. Let's talk about something you can do to ease the tension.

2. Trusting

Clients sometimes are afraid that the counselor is going to hurt them. One way to demonstrate this fear is to use a rubber band.

Counselor: Dan, I realize that you are having trouble trusting me, and somehow I have got to get you to understand that I am on your side and in no way am I going to intentionally hurt you. Perhaps this can help. I want you take one end of this rubber band. Now I am going to stretch it out *(counselor pulls on the other end until the rubber band is fully extended).*

In a few seconds, I am going to let go of the rubber band, but I am not going to hurt you. *(Client looks surprised and scared)... (The counselor slowly brings his hand toward the client's, thus reducing the tension on the rubber band, and then lets go.)*

Client: You're right. I thought for a second that you were going to hurt me. Then I didn't know what to think.

Counselor: How can we use this demonstration to get you to see that I am not going to hurt you?

Money

Clients who are battered or who allow someone to run all over them often feel worthless. One way to show them that their worth stays the same is by using money from your wallet.

Counselor: I want you to look at this. *(The counselor takes a $20 bill from his wallet.)* What is this?

Client: A 20 dollar bill.

Counselor: How much is it worth?

Client: Twenty dollars.

Counselor: *(Counselor crumples the bill, then steps on it, and kicks it. Then the counselor unfolds the bill.)* How much is it worth now?

Client: Uh, 20 dollars. *(The client pauses for a minute.)* I see what you are getting at. I could not see your point, but now I do. I really am not worth less because I've allowed this to happen.

Counselor: That's right!

Thick String

Clients often refer to problems that seem to have a "fuse" concept intertwined. They may talk about their fuses being too long or too short. Too long a fuse may be in reference to tolerating a bad relationship, so the client may need to see that she needs to shorten the fuse. Or if a client has too short a fuse, he may see that he needs to lengthen it. By using string of various lengths, the counselor can help the client visualize what he needs to do.

Counselor: Mario, we've only been talking 10 minutes, and you have told me how you've blown up at your kids, at your wife, and at work.

Client: I can't help it! It's who I am.

Counselor: That's not true at all. It's a fuse problem. I want you to look at these two fuses. *(The counselor pulls out two strings, one that is 2 inches in length and another that is 10 inches.)* You currently see yourself as having a short fuse. *(The counselor holds up the short fuse, and the client stares at it.)* I want you to know that through counseling, you can lengthen your fuse to this long. *(The client stares at the longer fuse.)*

Client: I do need to do something, or I am going to lose it all.

Counselor: I am glad to hear that you are motivated. Let's talk about how you developed your short fuse, and then we'll talk about ways of lengthening it. For now, I am going to put this small fuse on this little boy's chair, and I'm going to put the longer fuse on this "adult" or regular chair so that we can keep referring to them.

Poker Chips

Some clients walk around angry all the time and don't seem to understand why they often have bad days. To get the client to see how the odds are against his having good days when he is so angry, you can do the following:

Counselor: Pat, maybe I can help you to see what is going on. You say you don't understand, and yet it seems pretty clear to me. You want to have better days at school, at home, and at work; but you walk around angry most of the time. As a result, you get in some kind of argument or trouble. I've got some chips here. The red ones represent your being angry, and the white ones represent your being calm. I'm placing a number of chips in my hand; the majority are red since you are angry most days. *(Counselor places 10-12 red chips and 2-3 white chips in his hands.)* Close your eyes and pick a chip. Tell me what color it is. You'll see that the majority of the time you are going to pick a red one.

Client: Red.

Counselor: Pick another one.

Client: Red.

Counselor: Red chips mean that you are angry that day. Do you see how we have to work on your anger in order to change how your days go? Your anger, in a sense, creates how your life will go each day. We need to increase the number of white chips so that when you pick, the odds are that you will get a white chip instead of a red one.

Weights

Clients often feel weighted down by the "burdens" in their lives. To heighten their awareness of this weighted down feeling, I have used a variety of techniques.

Example 1

Counselor: Joyce, I want to show you what "superwoman" is doing to herself. Hold out both arms in front of you while I stack these books on them. *(Using heavy books or weights, the counselor places them one at a time on Joyce's arms.)* This first weight is taking care of your mother; the second is taking care of your father-in-law; the third is being a den mother for scouts.

Client: This is heavy.

Counselor: Keep them up, we're not done yet. You also are the choir director at church. Let's see, what else.

Client: I volunteer two mornings a week at the school and once a month at the shelter. *(Counselor adds two more books to the pile.)* I can't hold these up much longer.

Counselor: You have to—they are all important, and you don't want to give them up.

Client: No, seriously, my arms are hurting. It's too heavy.

Now the client is aware that she has more weight than she can handle, and the counselor can use the example for the remainder of the session to help her see that she has to let go of some things.

Example 2

Counselor: Chico, you never let go of a problem, and you keep adding more. I am going to put some books in this briefcase. Each book represents one of your problems. I'll start with four problems: mom, work, brother, and money. Hold your arm out. Now take the briefcase... *(Chico takes the briefcase and struggles to hold it up.)* No, keep your arm up.

Client: I can't do this. I don't want to do this!

Counselor: But the point is, you are doing this; and you are not making much progress to change any of this. Theoretically, you are coming to counseling to get rid of your problems; but so far, all you have done is describe them over and over again to me. I would suggest we start working on one of the problems so that you can lighten the load a little.

Puzzle

A child's puzzle can be used in a number of ways. You can have the client work the puzzle with a couple of pieces missing to highlight that she is trying to figure out something, but all the pieces aren't there. You can make reference to the problem being "like a puzzle, and all we have to do is get the pieces in the right place."

Counselor: I am going to give you this puzzle to work, and I want you to complete it as quickly as you can. *(The client starts working on the puzzle. There are a number of pieces missing.)*

Client: Hey, there are some pieces missing.

Counselor: That's true. Tell me what the picture is in this puzzle.

Client: I can't exactly because of the missing pieces. I can only guess.

Counselor: That's the point regarding your wife. You keep trying to get the picture, but it seems to me that there are too many missing pieces. What do you think?

Client: This is right! No wonder I can't figure this out. She says, "Give me space and don't ask questions; we're just good friends." Things just don't add up.

Counselor: I agree. What I want to get you to do is to at least accept that you don't have all the pieces.

Client: This helps a lot.

Video Tape

When clients seem stuck and destined to live this year just like last year, I have used video tapes to make a point.

Counselor: I want you to look at these two videos. This video is already made. It is a video of your life last year. We can't change it. The other video is about your life this year. Do you know what you are doing?... You are simply copying last year's tape. No changes in characters, no changes in activities, no changes! You have a choice; you can make a repeat, or you can make a very different video.

I use this analogy to keep the client focused on what he is doing and what he needs to do.

3 Use of Chairs in Counseling

In this chapter, I describe several ways an empty chair or chairs can be used in counseling. I discuss some of the Gestalt therapy uses of the empty chair, as well as some ways that chairs can be used in conjunction with Transactional Analysis and Rational-Emotive therapy. Chairs can be used to represent different people, different parts of a person, or different choices that a person is trying to make.

Use of an Empty Chair in Gestalt Therapy

Gestalt therapy often consists of heightening the client's awareness by bringing the issue into the present moment. By using an empty chair, the counselor can have the client dialogue with the person or parts of himself that he is having trouble with (Gladding, 1992; Passons, 1975; Perls, 1969). During Gestalt counseling the client is asked to move back and forth between seats. In this section, there are two examples showing this Gestalt approach to counseling. Many other examples in this chapter would be considered Gestalt, as well. These examples are brief, since the purpose is to demonstrate how the empty chair can be used and not to discuss Gestalt therapy in any detail. (See Passons, 1975 and Perls, 1969 for more information on how to use the empty chair in Gestalt therapy.) The use of "empty chair" work can be quite effective if the counselor's timing is right.

Example 1

Counselor: Rosie, instead of talking about your dad, I'd like you to act as if he is in this chair *(counselor pulls an empty chair in front of Rosie)*. What would you say to him?

Client: Dad, why can't you treat me like you do David?

Counselor: Now, sit here and be your dad and answer her.

Client: Quit bothering me with such nonsense.

Counselor: Change seats and be Rosie.

Client: It isn't nonsense, and you know it!

In Gestalt therapy, the counselor would usually have the client change seats back and forth a number of times, responding as herself and as her dad. This can be emotionally powerful and insightful.

Example 2

Counselor: I want to try something that may help you understand yourself better and why you do what you do. I want you to sit in this chair. *(The client sits in a chair in front of his original chair.)* Now I want you to be your fear of failure and tell yourself why you exist.

Client: Uh, well…

Counselor: *(Prompting the client)* I'm around to…?

Client: I'm around because I've always been here. There was much to be afraid of when I was growing up. You needed to be careful all the time at home.

Counselor: Change seats. What do you want to say to your fear of failure?

Client: That's right; there was a lot to be afraid of then, but this is now. I don't need you any more.

Counselor: Say that again.

Client: I don't need you!

Counselor: Say it one more time.

Client: I don't need you. I want to live. The world is not like it was when you were growing up. People can be trusted.

Example 3

In this example, the counselor is trying to help the client finish some "unfinished" business with her mother who committed suicide 3 years ago. It is the third session.

Counselor: Here's what I would like for you to do. I want you to bring your mother here by seeing her in this chair. What would you want to say to her?

Client: *(Looks at the chair for about 20 seconds and begins to cry.)* How could you leave me!? If you loved me, you would not have done this. Weren't I enough?

Counselor: Sit here and play your mom.

Client: *(After a 30-second pause)* Janey, I did love you, but I could not take the pain of what was happening in my life. It was not working.

Counselor: Change seats.

Client: Mom, I feel so guilty. Please forgive me for being so selfish. I should have seen your struggle. *(Cries harder.)*

Counselor: Sit here and say what your mom would say.

Client: Janey, I forgive you. It was my struggle. You were only 12 years old.

Counselor: Sit back over here. *(Client switches seats.)*

Client: Whew. *(Client comes out of the experience)*. Boy, I needed to hear that. This was powerful. I feel relieved or something. I'm not sure.

Counselor: I'll help you.

Getting Client to Talk to an Empty Chair

There are times when clients are hesitant to talk to an empty chair. One technique that I found to work almost all the time is for me to start in the chair.

Counselor: Sandy, let's try something. I want you to put your friend in this chair. What would you say to him?

Client: I don't think I can do this. I can't talk to an empty chair.

Counselor: Okay, let me sit in the chair and be your friend. What would you say?

Client: Why did you do this to me!

Counselor: *(The counselor gets out of the chair.)* Now sit here in your friend's seat and respond.

Client: *(Sitting in the friend's chair, thinking for a minute)* I really am sorry.

Counselor: Now sit in your seat and say some more.

The dialogue would continue with the client changing chairs. The client usually does not realize that she is now talking to an empty chair.

As I said in the beginning of this section, talking to an empty chair can be helpful in eliciting the client's deep-seated feelings. Studying Gestalt therapy has been very influential in my development as a therapist, and I encourage the reader who is not familiar with this approach to seek additional information.

Role Playing

With certain kinds of problems, an effective technique is the use of role playing or a combination of Gestalt therapy and role playing (Young, 1992). This involves the counselor's sitting in one of the chairs and playing one of the people or parts of a dialogue. It is important to remember that whenever you role-play some other person for the client, you want to be sure to have a good idea how to play the role. I ask, "Would he be loud or soft? Talk fast or slow? Would he be wordy or quick?" The advantage of having the client play both roles at first (using the Gestalt approach) is that the counselor can usually get a sense of the person she will be playing.

Counselor: I think I have a sense of how your boss will initially respond. Let's role-play where you are coming in to ask for the 3 days off, and I'll play your boss. I'll start. Duke, you said you wanted to see me.

Client: Yes. *(In a very hesitant voice)* I know I have only been here 5 weeks, but, uh, I need 3 days off.

Counselor: I don't think you get vacation until after 4 months.

Client: Well, what am I suppose to do, quit living? You're unfair!!

Counselor: Let's stop. No wonder you are afraid. I can see that you need some coaching in how to approach this. Did you tell your boss that your friends are counting on you to pay a fourth of the cost of the cabin and that you already had paid out $75?

Client: Well, no. I just know he is going to say no.

Counselor: No, you do not know that. You imagine it. Plus you did not give him any information. Let's do this again; but I will play you, and you will play your boss. Ready?

Choices

Many clients present problems that have to do with making a decision between two or more choices. By using different chairs to represent the choices, the counselor can help the client see more clearly what he is faced with (Passons, 1975; Perls, 1969).

Counselor: I am going to use these two chairs to represent the choices. This one represents divorce, and the other one represents staying married. Look at both of them. What do you see?

Client: I want them both.

Counselor: I know and, as you can see, there are two chairs. If there were only one chair or if we could mesh the two together like we can with playdough, there would be no problem. From all that you have said the last three sessions, there are two different paths you can take; and, whichever path you choose, you can't take the other path.

Client: Looking at the chairs makes it more real to me for some reason. I really am going to have to decide, aren't I?

Counselor: Yes, you are.

In the example above, the client is looking at the chairs. A variation would be to have the client sit in both seats and comment on how each one feels. When I use this technique, I often will pull a third seat between the other two.

Counselor: Now that you have sat in both seats, I want you to sit in this neutral seat between the two. What did you learn from sitting in both of them?

Client: I'm a mess. She wants to enjoy her life and to feel love and passion *(pointing to the chair on her left)*. *(Looking now to the chair on her right)* She is staying because of guilt, the kids, and what others will think. This helps me to see how I jumble the two.

37

The rest of the session can be conducted with her sitting in the middle chair. The presence of the chairs can help the client more clearly see her indecision.

In this example, more than one chair is used.

Counselor: Let me show you what you are up against. This chair represents your wife, and this chair represents the woman you are having the affair with. If you had to pick between the two women, not considering the kids, who would you pick?

Client: My lover.

Counselor: Now let me add to the picture. This chair represents your oldest child, and this little chair represents your 8-year-old. So now you are picking between your lover and the package deal of your wife and the two children. I say this because, from what you have said, your wife will take the kids and move a thousand miles away to her hometown. *(In front of the client on his right are three chairs and on his left is one chair.)*

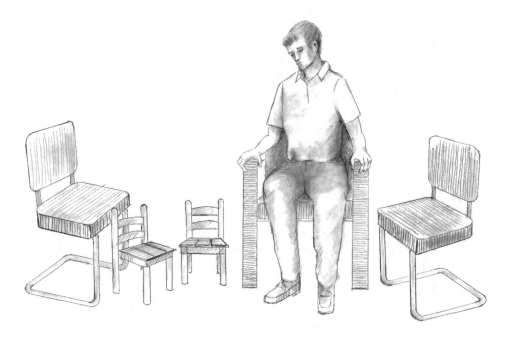

Throughout the session, the chairs can serve as a reminder of what the client's decision entails.

Small Child's Chair

In the first chapter, in the section on Essentials for Counseling, I included a child's chair because there are so many ways that a child's chair can be used to help make things clearer to the client. I often use the small chair in conjunction with Transactional Analysis. I have the client sit in the chair and comment from the Child ego state. The session frequently includes a dialogue between the client's Adult ego state and his Child ego state.

1. Wounded child

Much work is currently being done on healing the "wounded child" (Bradshaw, 1988; Love, 1990; Mellody, 1989). By having the small chair symbolize the wounded child, the client gets a chance to see that he is no longer a little boy or she is no longer a little girl.

Counselor: Tina, it's real clear to me that when you were a little girl, you were told some terrible things and were treated badly. Let us use this little chair to be the 8-year-old Tina. What do we need to do to help her heal those wounds? *(Client begins to cry as she looks at the chair.)*

Client: I don't know. There seems to be so much.

Counselor: Let me tell you what some clients have done in the past. *(Looking at the little chair)* Some have talked to the little girl and thanked her for getting her through the trauma.

>Some have talked to her about letting go of the hurt and
>shame. Some have sat in the little girl seat and talked
>about the pain she felt as a girl, and I played either
>counselor to the girl or the "parent she never had.".... What
>can we do to help you realize that you are okay and that
>you can have a good life?

No matter how you approach helping a client heal her wounded
child, the chair can prove to be very helpful in separating past from
present. Too, I want to emphasize that a small chair is much more
powerful than a regular chair when you are talking about the hurt child.

In working with incest survivors, the small chair has been
invaluable when trying to get the client to see that it was not her fault.
By being able to make reference to the chair, I feel the client gets some
sense that the little girl should not be blamed. In the example below, the
counselor has been discussing with the client that what happened was
not her fault. The chair has been used to represent the 9-year-old girl
who was molested by her father.

Counselor: *(Pointing to the small chair)* Abbey, how can you say that
she is responsible. How old was she?

Client: Nine through 14, but I should have known better.

Counselor: Look at her. She is a little girl who was doing what all girls
try to do. She was trying to please her daddy. She's a girl;
that is why we have a little girl's chair here and not a
woman's. You are a woman now, but she *(looking at the
chair)* was a frightened little girl. How do I get you to see
that it was not your fault!

Client: *(In a very warm, loving voice while looking at the little
chair)* It really wasn't your fault. You were young, and he
was the one who was wrong, not you.

2. The free (natural) child

Many therapists make reference to the inner child, the precious
child, or the free child (James & Jongeward, 1978; Stewart & Joines,
1987). The small chair can be used when talking about these with the
client. In the example below, the counselor has been discussing the
client's boring and uneventful life.

Counselor: Mike, there is a fun child inside of you; all of us like to
have fun. *(Pointing to the little chair)* How do we get you to
get in touch with that natural, free child?

Client: I don't know how to let him have fun *(looking at the chair
with tears in his eyes)*.

The counselor would focus on the topic of how to have fun by continuing to use the chair as a reminder of the client's free child. Once, I had a client ask to take the chair home with her for a day. She took the chair to the lake and down by the river with her to remind herself that the purpose that day was to have fun.

3. The hurt, angry, and/or not okay child

Often clients make reference to a hurt, angry, or "not okay" part of themselves. There will be times when the small chair can be used to symbolize this part. The counselor may refer to the chair or may actually have the client sit in the chair, depending on her approach to the problem.

Example 1

Counselor: Antonio, what are we going to do about this angry little boy who is inside of you? *(Pointing to the little chair.)*

Client: *(Stares at the chair)* He does get me in trouble all the time. What I'd like to do is this. *(Client picks the chair up and puts it in the closet.)*

Example 2

Counselor: Kim, I want you to sit here in the little chair and be the girl that is hurting. *(Client sits in the chair.)* Talk about what you are feeling now.

4. Letting go

I have used the small chair to symbolically show the client how she needs to leave her "little girl" in my office. (See illustration next page.) This technique can be used during or at the end of the session.

Counselor: Zoey, when you leave here each time, even when we have had a good session, you always take the "little girl" part of you with you. I would like for you to stand up. Let's assume we are ending today's session, and then you start to leave; but first pick up the chair. *(Client picks up the chair.)* Isn't this what you do? How do we get you to leave the "little girl" here?

Client: I'm not sure. I feel like I don't need her when I am here talking to you.

Counselor: Let's try this, Zoey. Say goodbye, and then walk past the chair and on out the door... *(Client walks out the door)* What was that like for you?

In the next example Roberto, who is 12 years old, has been talking to the school counselor about his fear of not being liked. The counselor has talked about Roberto's "little boy" part of himself.

Counselor: Roberto, we are at the end of our session today. I want you to decide if you need to take the "little boy" with you. Does it feel comfortable enough to leave him here today?

Client: *(Looking at the chair)* I want to leave him here.

Counselor: Good. What does that mean to leave your little boy here?

Client: It means that I won't react so much if they call me names and that I do have people that like me. They can't make me anything. I do that.

Counselor: That's great! I think you see the difference between the little boy part and the Adult part.

Standing on the Chair

Some clients present problems that have to do with their putting another person on a pedestal. To heightened the client's awareness of this, the counselor can stand on an empty chair.

Counselor:	This is what I am hearing. I am going to play her. *(Standing on a chair that is in front of the client)* Is this how it is? You have her way up here, don't you?
Client:	*(Looking up, sheepishly)* You're right. I do have her up there, sort of like what I did with my mother.
Counselor:	How do we get you to see her as a person and not as something bigger than life? Let's take a look at all this, including what you said about your mother.

Goals

An empty chair can be useful when talking about goals that the client has for herself.

Counselor:	Mona, you have told me your goals. Let's assume that this chair represents your goals. As I see it, your goals are way over here *(putting the chair a good distance from Mona)*.
Client:	I want to better myself.
Counselor:	I know you do, but honestly, how much movement have you made toward your goals? That chair is far away, and I want to help you move so that you can get there. *(Looking at the chair)* Do you believe you can get there?
Client:	I don't know.
Counselor:	I know that you will never get there if you don't move, and I do not feel that you are moving. Let's do something here today that moves you closer to your goal.
Client:	Like what can we do?
Counselor:	We can talk about how you always compare yourself to your sister. That's a habit that you need to break because you always end up putting yourself down.
Client:	You're right. That would probably get me half way to my goals.
Counselor:	I want you this session to be where you definitely feel that you've moved.

Distance

An empty chair can be used to symbolically represent another person and the distance that may be between that person and the client. By having the person symbolically there in the session, the counselor can show the client various things about the relationship.

Counselor: Suppose this chair represents your dad. You would like to be close to him, right? *(The counselor brings the chair next to the client)* How does this feel?

Client: Good!

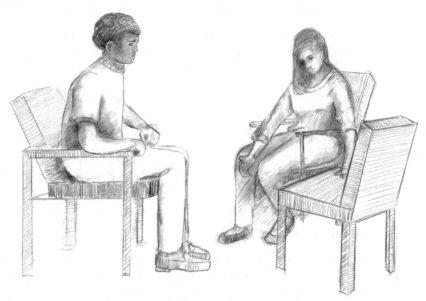

Counselor: But that's not how it is. From what you have said, your dad is more like this. *(The counselor turns the chair around and moves it far away from the client, and the client starts to cry.)*

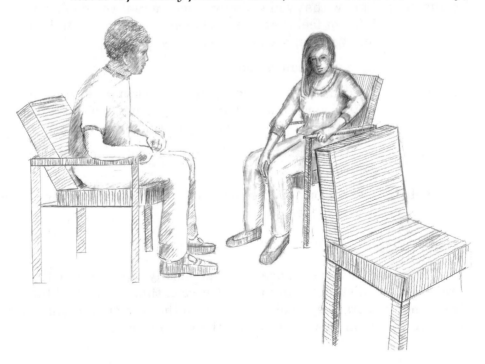

Client:	Why can't he be the other way!? I don't want him way over there.
Counselor:	Unfortunately, that's where he is, and I need to help you deal with where he is and not where you want him to be.

Crying

Many times during counseling the client will cry. Most of the time the counselor will want to be warm and supportive and just be with the client. There are times when the counselor may want to get the client out of her pain (Dinkmeyer, Dinkmeyer, & Sperry, 1987). One way to accomplish this is through the use of another chair.

In this example, the client has been talking about moving to another town and has started to cry. This is the third session regarding the pending move.

Client:	*(Crying)* I am scared.
Counselor:	Kari, I want you to do this. Move over to this seat and be the person who understands about moving and talk to the scared girl who is crying now. What would you say to her?
Client:	*(Moves to the other chair)* You know you'll be all right. It will be hard at first, but you will be able to make friends.
Counselor:	Do you want to switch back to the girl who was crying?
Client:	No, I'll stay here. It feels better here!

Then and Now

Two chairs can be used to drive home the point regarding something that happened in the past and how the client needs to be in the present.

Counselor:	I want you to look at these two chairs. Now what year is this?
Client:	1992. *(The counselor writes 1992 on a sheet of paper and tapes it to the chair so the client can see it.)*
Counselor:	What year did all that happen?
Client:	1980. *(The counselor writes 1980 on a sheet of paper and tapes it to the other chair.)*
Counselor:	What year again did you say this is?
Client:	1992.
Counselor:	Which chair are you living your life from, 1980 or 1992?
Client:	*(Thinks for a minute)* I think I'm still in 1980.
Counselor:	Go sit there for a minute.

Rational and Irrational

Counselors who use RET can use two chairs to represent the rational and irrational points of view.

Example 1

Counselor: I want you to have this chair represent the irrational you, and the other chair to be the rational you. I want the two to have a dialogue, and we'll hear which is the strongest. Which one do you want to start with?

Client: The rational one.

Counselor: Okay, sit here. What do you want to say to her?

Client: I know he is not good for me. He drinks, and he sees other girls. I want a better life than he can give me. So even though it will hurt for a while, I need to break up.

Counselor: Change seats.

Client: But he's more fun than any guy you have been with. He's says he'll quit drinking and get a job as soon as the summer is over. You're getting older and may not find anyone.

Counselor: Change.

Client: That's nonsense. I am only 23, and he's more than likely not going to go to work. He's not what I want. He's fun at times, and at other times he makes me miserable. Oops, that's right, you taught me that he doesn't make me miserable. I make myself miserable by what I'm telling myself.

Counselor: Good. Any insight?

Client: Both parts are strong. I want to be in the rational chair; but I am, I hate to admit it, more familiar with the irrational chair. I think I've lived most of my life from that chair.

Example 2

Counselor: Sit in this seat and say what you just said.

Client: Because I didn't get selected as cheerleader, it means my life is ruined.

Counselor: Now sit back over here *(pointing to the chair)*. Can you dispute that statement? Is what she is saying true?

Client: Well, it is not exactly true.

Counselor: What is true? I want you to get to where you tell yourself things that are true. *(Pointing to the chair)* She makes up all kinds of things, whereas you want to learn to tell yourself the truth about events. What is the truth about not getting selected as cheerleader?

Example 3

Counselor: Don, we have two chairs here, one is the rational you, and one is the irrational you regarding being adopted. Which one do you want to be?

Client: I believe that I'm less than others and not lovable.

Counselor: That would qualify for the irrational chair. Would you know what to say from the rational chair?

Client: I guess not.

Counselor: Here's what we'll do. I'll sit in the rational chair, and you sit in the irrational chair, and we'll have a discussion about the meaning of adoption.

Client: *(Head hanging down)* I don't know who I am. I can't ever be much.

Counselor: That's nonsense. You do know who you are. There's only one fact here. You were adopted. Who you are now is your history. That's you, and you can become whatever you set your mind to becoming.

Client: No. I wouldn't want to become anyone where I would have to tell people I was adopted.

Counselor: Look, there's nothing wrong with being adopted. Let's pause here. Is any of this making sense?

Client: There sure are the two parts. But to be honest, until I came here, I thought there was only the one part. I still am going to need lots of work to believe the rational part. It does make some sense though.

I strongly believe a counselor can be much more impactful when she adds the use of chairs to her counseling, because chairs can make therapy clearer and more concrete.

4 Use of Movement in Counseling

In this chapter, I discuss how the counselor can use creative movement techniques that involve the client, the counselor, or both getting up from their seats and performing some activity that is relevant to the counseling. Although there is a type of therapy known as dance therapy (Feder & Feder, 1981; Levy, 1988), I do not discuss it in this book. The focus here is on the creative use of movement during the counseling session because movement activities make counseling more concrete, interesting, visual, experiential, and energized.

Evaluation of Progress

For various reasons counselors will, at times, have their clients assess their progress. One creative way to do this is to have clients stand up and position themselves according to how much progress they think they have made during counseling.

In the example below, the counselor feels that Chet's progress has slowed down, and the counselor wants to do something to dramatize this for him.

Counselor: Chet, I'd like you to stand up. If where you are standing is where you were when you started counseling 6 weeks ago, and this line (*counselor draws an imaginary line on the floor about 8 feet in front of him*) represents the goals we talked about, how much progress have you actually made?

Client: (*Thinks for a moment, then moves about 2 feet*) I'm about here, I think.

Counselor: Yes, and you have been there for about the last 3 weeks. Put one foot forward, representing some movement we can make today. (*The client puts his right foot forward.*)... What does your foot represent?

Fear of Changing

Changing is a frightening thing for many clients. Some clients, even though they want to change, resist it. They hold onto what is familiar (Campos, 1988; Steiner, 1974).

Example 1

The counselor has been working to get the client to reach the goals that they established.

Counselor: Sung, let me show you what you are doing. Let's assume the chair over there represents your goals. Now I want you to grab the chair you are in and hold onto it very tight. *(The counselor stands and extends his hand)* As I reach for you to try to help you move to the "goals" chair, look at what happens. Rather than letting go, you hold on tight to what is familiar.

Client: I really do want to change, but I guess I am afraid.

Counselor: That's right. I'd like you to loosen your grip and gently take my hand... Now I am going to help you move slowly to the other chair. Counseling is about my helping you to change *(client slowly moves to the other chair).*

Client: I do have to trust you and, I guess, trust myself. I like it better in this seat.

The client now has a better understanding of the counseling process and what she needs to do. Throughout the session, reference can be made to the chairs and the movement between them.

Example 2

This example depicts another way that the client resists change.

Counselor: Steve, I want to show you what you are doing. We work in counseling to get you to move from where you are to where you want to be *(counselor pulls up a second chair).* Here's what I'd like you to do. I want you to sit where you are, then move to this other chair and, as soon as you sit in this chair, quickly move back to your original chair. Do this two or three times. *(The client does this.)*

Client: I am not sure what your point is.

Counselor: Think about it.

Client: *(After a long pause)* I think I've got it. You're saying that when I do make changes, I don't stay with them very long.

Counselor: That's right. Say some more.

Example 3

The counselor has realized that the client is either afraid to make changes or wants the counselor to do most of the work. The counselor decides to use a creative movement technique.

Counselor: Carl, I want you to stand up. *(The counselor stands in front of Carl about 8 feet away with his hand stretched out.)* Standing where you are, reach out and take my hand.

Client: *(The client reaches out but is too far away to take the counselor's hand.)* I can't reach you.

Counselor: That's right. And I can't go any farther. It's up to you to move so that we can make contact. What can you do to move so that we meet? My hand is out.

Example 4

A variation of this would be to have the counselor move closer and the client slap the hand. In this example, the counselor has been working with a resistant teenager and wants to try something different in hopes of engaging Jerry.

Counselor: Jerry, let me show you what you do here in counseling. Let's both stand up. *(The counselor is about 4 feet from the client with his hand extended.)* I hold out my helping hand, and do you know what you do?

Client: No, what?

Counselor: Think about it. My hand is out each week, and what do you do?

Client: I don't take your hand. Is that what you mean?

Counselor: You actually do more than that. You slap my hand. I'll put my hand up; now you slap it. *(Client does this.)* Do it again.

Client: Hey, man, don't take it personally...

Counselor: I don't. I do want to help you, but I need your cooperation. What do you think?

By doing this demonstration, the counselor may be able to achieve a breakthrough. At the very least, the client will think more about his resistance.

Feeling Helpless

There are some clients who want the counselor to do all the work. They either feel helpless, or they act helpless.

Example 1

Counselor: Andrea, I don't think you realize what you are doing. You say you want to move to that other chair, but you keep looking to me to do it for you. You do not do any of the things we agree on during the week. Here's the image I have. You are in your seat, and you want me to come and more or less pick you up and carry you to the other seat. *(The counselor comes over to the client and acts out trying to pick up the client.)* You are not that helpless, and counseling can never be successful if I am doing all the work.

Client: Is it really this bad?

Counselor: You tell me. How hard are you working to change?

By showing the client what she is doing, the counselor hopes to get her to see that she is going to have to do the work.

The next two examples show how the counselor can use a creative movement technique to dramatize how the client is not fighting very hard to change. When using the techniques described in these examples, the counselor needs to be sure that his timing is right.

Example 2

Counselor: I need to demonstrate for you what you are doing. Let me stand behind you... Now when you try to get up and move to the chair with your goals in it, here's what happens. Go ahead and get up. *(The client starts to rise, and the counselor presses down on both shoulders. The client immediately sits back down.)* Do you see what you just did?

Client: No, what?

Counselor: You gave up as soon as you met resistance. That's what you are doing with your life, and that is why you are not making the progress you want. Let's do it again, but this time don't give up. Fight through the resistance. *(The client attempts to get up again, meets resistance, but this time fights to get up, and moves to the chair designated as her goals.)*

Client: *(Breathing hard from the struggle)* I like it better here. I now see how much effort this is going to take.

Example 3

This example is similar to the previous one, except the counselor acts out the scene differently. In this case, the counselor has the goals in another chair opposite the client. The counseling session has centered around how much the client wants to reach his goals. The client says he wants to, but so far he has made very little progress. Kareem is the kind of guy who talks a good game but really does very little.

Counselor: Kareem, you say you want to reach the goals, right?

Client: That's right.

Counselor: Are you willing to try hard to reach those goals over there?

Client: That's why I'm here.

Counselor: Okay. *(Moving so that he is now standing in front of Kareem.)* I want you to try to get to your goals.

Client: But you are in my way.

Counselor: If you want your goals bad enough, you can get around me.

Client: *(Starts to get up. The counselor gently pushes him back in his seat.)* I can't.

Counselor: Do you see what you are doing?

Sometimes the client will decide to try to move the counselor out of the way, and a struggle will take place. The counselor must be prepared for this. It is also important that the client not feel that he is fighting the counselor but rather is fighting the parts of himself that holds him back.

Movement Along Maslow's Hierarchy of Needs

Abraham Maslow (1968) set forth a hierarchy of needs. He theorized that human beings have different needs and these needs more or less follow an order, starting first with physiological needs. If those needs are not being met, then they will be a priority. If a person's physiological needs are being met, then other needs will motivate him. Maslow's theory is one that I feel all counselors should be familiar with, and I encourage you to read more about Maslow if you have not been exposed to this theory. His hierarchy of needs are as follows:

1. physiological

2. safety and security

3. loving and belonging

4. self-esteem

5. self-actualizing

I have used this theory as a way to demonstrate for a client what is happening in her life. I have the five needs written out on separate sheets of paper, and I lay the sheets on the floor in a line about 2 feet apart. I very briefly tell the client what each one means; then I have her stand up.

Counselor: I want you to position yourself where you think you were 3 years ago.

Client: Three years ago I was here at "safety and security."

Counselor: And now?

Client: Having gone back to school and finding out that I can do college work, I am heading toward "self-esteem." I think I have one foot there already, but my need to be liked still is pulling on me. *(The client positions herself between "love and belonging" and "self-esteem." She pauses, obviously thinking...)*

Counselor: What are you thinking?

Client: This helps a lot. I can see where I have been and where I want to go. I want you to help me get there.

Feeling Pulled

In the above example, the client mentioned that her need to be liked was still "pulling on her." An extension of the use of the hierarchy can be to let the client experience the "pull."

Example 1

Counselor: Cheryl, you are moving, but let me show you what happens as you move toward self-esteem. Your parents and your husband don't understand, and they don't like the way you are changing. I am going to play them, and I want you to start to move toward self-esteem. *(The client starts to move, and the counselor grabs one of her arms and tries to pull her back.)*

Client: You got it! This is how it feels. What do I do about it?

This demonstration allows the client to experience some of what she feels is happening to her. The use of "pulling" does not have to be in conjunction with Maslow's hierarchy. The next two examples show other ways in which clients feel pulled.

Example 2

Counselor: Bob, I want you to stand and start to move toward your goals; and as you do, I am going to be behind you, trying to pull you back. *(Bob starts forward, and the counselor pulls him back.)*

Client: This sure is how it feels.

Counselor: We need you to identify your "pulls" and to get you strong enough to break free of them.

Example 3

Counselor: Let's try to set up how this is for you. This chair is going to represent you. *(The counselor places a chair between her and the client, who is a 9-year-old boy.)* I am going to play your mom, and you are going play your dad; and each of us is going to try to pull the chair to us. Okay, pull!! *(The two tug very hard on the chair.)*

Client: *(After some rigorous tugging)* I do feel pulled. I feel sorry for the chair.

Counselor: If there had been another person here, I would have put you in the chair, but I think you see my point.

Client: I don't want to be in the middle of their divorce, and I don't want to be pulled.

Counselor: We have to get you out of the middle. Let's talk about what you are going to have to do to stay out of the middle.

Paths

Clients will sometimes discuss problems that relate to choosing a different way to live. Often teenagers who are heading down a path that leads to nowhere can be helped if this is acted out in some form.

Counselor: Andy, I'd like you to stand here in the middle of the room. You seem to be faced with the decision of which path to take. This path is staying in school, and this one is quitting school. *(Client walks down the "quit school" path.)* If you go that way, where will you end up?

Client: I don't know. I just know that school is a drag.

Counselor: But where does the path lead you? Isn't that the question we have to address? Look at the other path, where does it lead?

There may be times when you will want to further dramatize the different paths by having the client start to walk down the "positive" path, and then you start to pull him off the path.

Movement along paths also can be utilized when trying to get clients to see the value of using a support group such as AA.

Counselor: So you feel that you can quit drinking by yourself even though you have tried many times in the past to quit.

Client: This time is different! I am determined to do it!

Counselor: I'd like to show you something. Let's stand up. I'd like you to walk your recovery path, which is one of doing it by yourself. Assume that your path is about 8 feet long. I am going to represent alcohol and stand next to the recovery path. Just walk up and down that path. *(After the client passes by the counselor once or twice, the counselor grabs him hard and pulls him off the path. The client is shocked and confused.)*
That's what I believe is going to happen to you if you don't use the support of AA and work a program. Now if you take this other path which represents working a recovery program that includes counseling, working the 12 steps, and AA, you will probably feel more comfortable. Walk along this path. *(The path is out of the reach of the counselor, so he does not have to worry about being grabbed.)*

Client: This does feel safer.

Counselor: Getting support and help is okay and necessary. Let's talk some more about this because I want you to understand the value of working a program.

Variations of this type of movement activity can be used with people who are not in recovery but who are in need of support for getting over a divorce or other major loss.

Position on a Continuum

Having a client position himself along a continuum can be thought provoking and can serve to energize the session by having the client move around.

Example 1

Counselor: Leslie, I'd like you to stand here in the middle of the room. If the wall on your left is "wanting to date men" and the wall on your right is "wanting to date women," where would you put yourself?

Client: When you put it this way, it is hard to say. I feel in the middle.

Counselor: That's okay. There is no right or wrong answer. I'm just trying to help you see where you are.

Example 2

Counselor: Jay, let me get you to stand up. If the wall on your left is getting married and the wall on your right is breaking the engagement, where would you position yourself.

Client: *(Client thinks for a minute, then moves close to the wall on his right.)* It doesn't feel good being here, but this is what I want to do.

Counselor: I understand that. Let's talk about your choice.

Example 3

Counselor: Billy, this wall represents fighting and being a tough guy at school, being in trouble all the time, and not doing any of your work. This other wall represents doing the work, staying out of trouble, and going on to college. Where do you want to be?

Client: Well, I don't want to be a "goody-two-shoes."

Counselor: Let's say that would be the wall. The question is where along this continuum between the walls do you want to be?

Example 4

Client: I did have one beer as I watched the hockey game. I just wanted to see if I could do it, and I did. No problem. It did feel good to be back in the bar.

Counselor: How about going to the AA meetings?

Client: Well, I haven't been going so often. In fact, I've only gone to one in the last 2 weeks, but I don't think I need to go too often.

Counselor: Have you been talking with your sponsor?

Client: Not much lately. I don't think he understands.

Counselor:	Stand up here. *(Client stands in the middle of the room.)* If that wall represents working your recovery program and this wall represents relapse, where would you have put yourself a month ago?
Client:	A month ago, huh, let's see. I would have been right close to the wall of recovery. I was going to four meetings a week and talking to my sponsor every day.
Counselor:	That's right. Now where would you put yourself today?
Client:	Being honest, I'm about in the middle.
Counselor:	That's probably close, but you need to turn around and face the relapse wall, because you are looking more at relapse than recovery. What do you think?
Client:	I guess I didn't think about it like this. More than anything, I do not want to go back to the way I was. I am not working much of a program, am I?
Counselor:	True. And to stay sober, you have to work a recovery program.

Obstacles

Many times clients do not make progress toward their goals due to various obstacles. It may be helpful to create a visual image of this by setting up the goals and then putting all kinds of obstacles in the way. The counselor can use various objects in her office, such as chairs, the trash can, tables, lamps, etc.

Counselor:	Tandy, I want you to walk to the far corner of the room. You've been talking about wanting to move from where you are to here *(a place in the room that is about 10 to 15 feet away)*. Let me put some things in your way *(counselor puts objects between the client and her goals)*. Let's name these obstacles and then figure how to get over them, around them, or through them.

This dramatization can help the client see what she needs to do, and the counselor can make reference to the obstacles throughout the session. Often I have done the rest of the session with the client standing, looking at the obstacles, and talking about them.

Going in Circles

Certain clients appear as though they are going in circles or may even say they feel that they are going in circles. To highlight this, the counselor can ask the client to stand and walk in circles.

Counselor: Rex, let me show you what we're doing. Stand here behind me and follow me as I walk around. *(The counselor goes in circles with the client following.)*

Client: *(Laughing)* I'm going in circles, right?

Counselor: That's right.

Client: I do need to get going in some direction, or I won't get anywhere. Thanks for showing me what I was doing.

Standing in the Corner

A creative way to dramatize for a client how he is not seeing his options is to have the client go stand in the corner of the room.

Counselor: You're not seeing your options.

Client: There are none.

Counselor: No, that's not true. You are not seeing your choices, and then each week you report that you have had a bad week. Here's what you do. I want you to go stand there in the corner and face the corner. *(The client does this.)* Now, go forward.

Client: I can't, there's no place to go.

Counselor: *(The counselor walks over near the client, using an encouraging voice)* I hope you realize that you can go lots of places if you turn around. If you stay in the corner, your life isn't going to go anywhere. Just glance around, and then turn back to the corner. What's that like?

Client: There's something to see if I turn around.

Counselor: You have a whole life in front of you. You are only 20 years old. Let's do whatever it takes to get you out of the corner.

Movement Between Chairs

In the previous chapter, I discussed the Gestalt technique of using two chairs to help a person make a decision. A variation of this technique is to have the person move between the chairs but not say anything. This technique would be used when the client has already discussed at length the pro's and con's of each choice and just continues to go over and over the same material.

Counselor: I want you to sit here. *(The client moves; and just as she sits down, the counselor says...)* Now sit back over here. *(Client moves and sits for a second.)* Now move again...

Now move again. Just move on your own. *(The client does this for two or three more times.)*

Client: Can I talk from one of the positions?

Counselor: I don't think it will help you unless you have something new to say. Why do you think I had you do this?

Client: Probably to get me to see how I'm just bouncing back and forth and getting nowhere.

Counselor: You believe you are working on the problem because your mind is active. But actually you are just rehashing both sides. Let's do one more thing that should drive this point home. I want you to sit in both seats at the same time.

Client: What?... I can't... I think I'm starting to see that I've got to let go of the notion that I'm going to be able to do both. Also, I see there really is no easy or even right answer.

Role Reversal

Role reversal, or changing places with the client, can be used for a number of reasons (Dinkmeyer, Dinkmeyer, & Sperry, 1987; Nugent, 1990). It gives the client a chance to see himself. It can cause him to come up with responses to his concerns. It can even help him understand how hard the counseling is for the counselor.

Example 1

Counselor: Louie, I've got an idea. Let's switch seats; and I am going to be you, and you are going to be me. *(The two switch places. The counselor takes on the body posture of Louie: head down, arms folded.)*

Client: You want me to be counselor, right. *(Counselor nods.)* Louie, how's it going today?

Counselor: *(Looking down)* Okay.

Client: What would you like to talk about?

Counselor: Nothing.

Client: *(After some silence)* Do I really look like that? That's pathetic.

Example 2

The counselor is trying to get Tami to talk about how she feels about her father's not coming to the school play that she was in.

Counselor: It is obvious that it is bothering you.

Client: I don't want to talk about it, okay?

Counselor: Why don't we try something different. Let's change seats, and you be the counselor and ask me questions. *(They change seats.)*

Client: Why does it bother you so much that he didn't come?

Counselor: I don't know.

Client: Is it because you believe that he doesn't care about you since you are not his real daughter?

As you can see, by using the role reversal technique, some important material may surface.

Values

With teenagers and adults, conflict often arises when the client decides to do something outside of his parents' value system.

Counselor: So you are saying that you don't feel that it is wrong for you to be dating someone of another race, but your parents do. Let me show you what I see is happening. Hold your hands up about 12 inches apart...That represents your values. Now I am going to use my hands to represent your parents' values. *(Counselor holds his hands up, about 6 inches apart, and puts his hands between the clients' hands.)* Your parents want you to fit in their value system, so they are trying to squeeze you back. *(Counselor puts his hands outside the client's and tries to squeeze the client's hands. The client resists.)*

Client: That's right. Why don't they just stretch?

Counselor: Let's do that. I'll put my hands back between yours and resist... Do you see what the battles are about now?

Client: Boy, do I. This makes it so clear!

Counselor Movement

Many of the examples above involved both the counselor and the client moving. Below are three situations where only the counselor moves in order to make contact with the client or to make a point.

Example 1

The client is a person who feels so ashamed of herself that she just sits and stares at the floor, never making eye contact. The counselor has seen her twice and feels that there is some rapport between the two of them. The counselor knows that the client could benefit by making contact with him instead of just watching those "movies in her mind," so he decides to try something.

Counselor: Patti, I'd like you to try to look up at me.

Client: I can't. I know you think I am awful, too.

Counselor: No, you think that of yourself; I don't, and I want you to look at me so that you can see that I don't think you are awful.

Client: I can't. I just can't look up.

Counselor: *(Using a very warm, kind voice)* Well, I'm going to try something else then *(moving slowly to the floor right in front of the client)*. I'll come down here so that I can look at you. Please let me in. I know I can be of help because I know you are not the bad person you think you are... How does this feel?

Client: A little awkward.

Counselor: That's fine. We'll just sit like this for a while. I like making eye contact with you.

Client: Me, too. Thanks.

Example 2

The counselor has come to realize that the client "hangs" on her every word. The client is always looking for the counselor's approval and, therefore, stares at her. The counselor has talked to the client about this, but she still stares at her. To break up this pattern, the counselor has decided to do something different.

Counselor: Wanita, you are still cueing off me. *(In a kind voice)* I am going to move my chair behind you so that you cannot see me, and we are going to do this session and perhaps the next one like this. I want you to learn to talk without paying so much attention to how I am reacting.

Example 3

Even though in another chapter I discussed the idea of the counselor standing on a chair, I want to mention it again, because it is a very useful technique.

Counselor: I don't think you realize what you are doing to yourself. *(Standing on a chair in front of the client)* You put your sister way up here. No wonder you are afraid of her.

Client: *(Looking up)* This is how it feels, and it sure doesn't feel good. How do I knock her off the chair?

Counselor: It really isn't about knocking her off the chair, but rather it is about how you give your power away. Let's talk about you and feeling powerless. When did you first feel so powerless?

Example 4

Many clients feel as though they are always working hard to get good grades on imaginary life "report cards."

Counselor: Let me show you what you are doing to yourself. You believe that you get report cards from your boss, your husband, your parents, and many other people. Let's take your husband. *(The counselor stands on the chair and takes some cards and writes on them, "Sandy's report cards.")* From what you are saying, you check with him to find out your grade on how you do with the kids, the dishes, the lawn, and almost everything else. He's up here with these report cards.

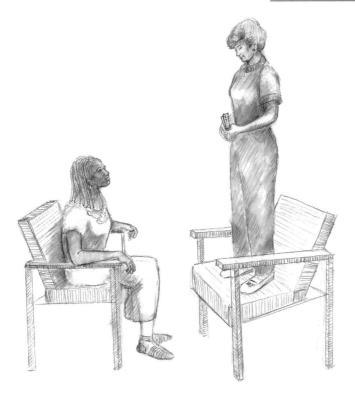

Client: Boy, how vivid. And true. I have done this all my life! I used to get sick every grading period in school, and in many ways I still am. No wonder I have ulcers and am anxious all the time. What do I do?

Counselor: No more school. No more report cards!

Client: I really do see that I need to change this.

5 Use of Writing and Drawing in Counseling

In this chapter, I describe many different ways that writing and drawing can be used in counseling. I describe how these techniques can be used both during the session and between sessions. The definition of writing that I am using is a very simple one: anything that is written by the counselor or the client on a small pad, a large newsprint pad, or a wipe board. The definition of drawing is also simple: anything drawn by either the counselor or the client.

It should be noted that there are some therapies that rely extensively on writing (McKinney, 1976; Progoff, 1975). Also, there are some therapists who practice "art therapy" (Riley, 1987; Wadeson, 1987). I do not address these approaches to counseling since they are covered elsewhere. Instead, I offer some unique, simple, creative, effective ways to use writing and drawing in counseling.

In the first chapter, I listed a large pad or wipe board as an essential for counseling. It is a rare session that I do not go to my wipe board and write, list, or draw something. I do this to focus the client, to make the content more concrete, or to provide some kind of visual picture for the client.

Ratings

One of the most helpful techniques to use when the client is discussing various people or aspects in his life, such as his marriage, his job, or his week, is to have him rate the person or thing on a 1-10 scale. Usually, showing this can be more impactful than just saying it out loud.

Example 1

Counselor: I want you to rate how your life has been this last month. If 10 is wonderful and 1 is terrible, what would you give your life?

Client: Overall, about a 6. *(Counselor has written out a vertical scale with 10 at the top and 1 at the bottom. He marks a 6 on the scale.)*

Counselor: How do we get you next month to move from a 6 to an 8 or 9? What is between a 6 and an 8 for you? *(Counselor marks an 8 on the scale and writes the name of the next month.)*

Client: *(Staring at the scale)* I do want to move up. I want better than a 6.

Example 2

The client has been describing her marriage as terrible, and yet she keeps hoping for it to get better. The counselor decides to do a graph of the last 5 years of her marriage. (See graph below.)

Counselor: Let's do something that might help you. We're going to make a graph of your marriage. I am going to ask you to rate your marriage over the last 5 years. Five years ago what would you rate your marriage on a 1-10 scale with 10 being great and 1 being terrible?

Client: Five years ago... it was about 6; that's when Janie was born. *(The counselor marks on the large pad a 6 above "five years.")*

Counselor: Four years ago?

Client: A 5 *(Counselor marks the graph)*.

Counselor: Three years?

Client: Still a 5.

Counselor: Two years?

Client: That's when his affair started. It was a 3.

Counselor: This past year?

Client: It's gotten worse. A 2.

Counselor: And presently?

Client: A 2 or a 1.

```
10
 9
 8
 7
 6        x
 5                    x         x
 4
 3                                      x
 2                                               x
 1                                                        x
      Five years ago  Four    Three     Two      One    Present
```

Counselor: Tell me how you can see any hope of a good life with this man.

Client: Well, it could get better.

Counselor: Sure, but look at the graph. What does the data say compared to what your heart says?

Client: *(Starts to cry)* It's been hell. Seeing it in black and white makes it seem so hopeless... It isn't going to work, I can see that now.

Example 3

The counselor has been talking with a teenager about how hurt he is over his parents' behavior towards him. The counselor decides to use a rating to drive home her point.

Counselor: Ted, I am going to list your mom, your dad, and you up here. We're going to rate each one in terms of being psychologically healthy and happy. How would you rate your mom, the woman who is on her fourth marriage in the last 6 years?

Client: She's not happy at all. She's about a 3.

Counselor: Let's rate your dad, the guy you see five or six times a year and who is drunk three or four of those times.

Client: He's maybe a 4. Sometimes a 1 when he is drunk.

Counselor: How would you rate yourself?

Client: Much of the time I feel an 8, except when something happens with Mom or Dad.

Counselor: Look at your ratings: Mom – 3
Dad – 1-4
Ted – 8

Counselor: If your parents were 7s or 8s or 9s, I'd say listen to them because they are your parents. But if you listen to people who are functioning at a level way below you, you more than likely are going to be told some pretty screwed up things.

Client: You've got that right! *(Looks at ratings.)*

Counselor: Please understand. I'm not saying to quit loving your parents. Rather, I am saying that unhappy parents often say very unkind things to their children. If an 8 listens to a 3, he almost always will be hurt or disappointed.

Example 4

The client wants to quit being so angry at her 19-year-old son who sits around the house and does nothing. She has described to the counselor in detail how she comes home from work every day and yells at him.

Counselor: Doris, maybe this will help you to get a perspective. On a 1-10 scale, how would you rate your son as far as how he is doing as a 19-year-old? A 10 for a person his age would be someone who is in college or trade school or the military or working and who is very cooperative and appreciative. A 1 would be someone who is doing drugs, selling drugs, stealing from you, or something like that. Your son is neither a 1 or a 10. What rating would you give him?

Client: Gosh, I don't want to rate him. I want him to be a 9 or a 10.

Counselor: I know, but he's not a 9 or 10. What you rate him does not mean he has to be this way forever; it means this is how you see him now.

Client: Well, he's a 3 or 4. He's not doing anything good, but he's also not doing anything terrible. He mainly sits around and watches t.v.

Counselor: Let's give him a 4. *(The counselor marks a 4 on the scale.)* Now, do you come home in the evening with the under-standing that your son is a 4, or do you come home with the idea that he should be an 8, and then you get mad when his behavior is that of a 4?

Client: I sure don't come home saying he's a 4. He should do things that he says he's going to do, such as going for that interview!

Counselor: Now wait, let's look at our rating. You have him as a 4. I would say that a person who is a 4 very often doesn't do what he says he is going to do or should do. Would you agree?

Client: *(Smiling)* Well, when you put it that way, no; a 4 would usually not go for an interview. Are you saying I should not expect anything of him?

Counselor: I'm saying that I don't think your expectations are in line with reality. I'm trying to get you to see that you are choosing to let your "4" son live with you, and then you come home each day mad that he's not at least a 7. If you accepted that for now he is a 4, do you think you would get as mad?

Client: No, I guess not. Seeing that 4 up there helps.

Example 5

Counselor: I want to list the different things you look for in a partner, and then we'll rate Filip on these characteristics. What's on your list?

Client: I would want the person to have a good work history. He'd be a good father. He's considerate. Sexually he's fun. Nice looking. Trustworthy.

Counselor: Look at this list. We may add some more, but let's just rate these for now. How would you rate Filip on a 1-10 scale.

   Work History
   Potential as a Parent
   Considerate
   Good Sexually
   Nice Looking
   Trustworthy

Client: On two of them he's a 10–his looks and sex. *(The counselor writes the numbers beside the characteristic.)* He's much better than any other man I have been with. On the others, he doesn't do so well. Work history is weak–he hates his job now and says he's going to quit. Potential as a parent–how do I know; he says he's not sure if he wants children.

Counselor: Let's give those two a number. What would they be?

Client: Work would be no more than a 4. Parent would be 4 or 5. Really a question mark.

Counselor: What about considerate and trustworthy?

Client: Those aren't very good either. I have already caught him in a number of lies, and sometimes he's over 2 hours late and doesn't even call. He's a 4 on each of these.

Counselor: I want you to look at this and tell me what you see.

Work History	4
Potential as a Parent	5
Considerate	4
Good Sexually	10
Nice Looking	10
Trustworthy	4

Client: I don't like what I see. The important characteristics are very low. I can't marry someone because of their looks and sex. Those things are important, but not that important. No wonder I've felt uneasy about this relationship. It's so helpful looking at the big picture. I can't deny the numbers. I don't even have family background, religion, and drinking habits up there, and they are on my list. Those would not get good ratings either unfortunately.

Goals

Making a list of the client's goals can be helpful in numerous ways. The counselor can make reference to them when the client starts talking about something that is contradictory to the goals.

Example 1

Counselor: Now wait a minute, look at your goals. (*Points to them.*) What did you say was your top goal?

Client: To be happy.

Counselor: Now explain to me how you can be happy if you go live at home. I know you feel like you "owe" your parents something, but how can going to live there help you to reach your top goal or your second goal which is to enjoy your job?

Client: I can't be happy there.

Counselor: Look at your list of goals… Do you want to change them.

Client: (*Client stares at his list.*) No, I believe in my list. It's good to have that goal written up there. I feel I have to be more honest.

Example 2

Counselor: Let's take a look at what your goals are for the next 2 years.

Client: Get a job. That's the key to it all.

Counselor: Maybe. What else is important for you during the next 2 years?

Client: Well, I want to get started on my master's degree, and I want to start exercising. You know, as I see you write that, I realize that I do not like myself with this extra 30 pounds.

Counselor: Are there more?

Client: Looking up there, I keep thinking of things. I want to get more at peace with my religious beliefs, and I want to develop some more interesting friends.

Counselor: Look at the list here.

> Get a Job
>
> Begin Master's Work
>
> Exercise–Lose Weight
>
> Peace With My Religion
>
> Make New Friends Who Are Interesting

Client: I wonder why it is that seeing them written makes me feel like they are more real than just saying them out loud.

Counselor: I'm not sure. I'm glad that this is making you think. I'll put this list up each week you come, and we'll use it to talk about your progress.

Client: That will be good because I need something to keep me on track.

Stroke Economy

TA therapists use the term "strokes" to describe a person's positive and negative interactions. A term that is used to describe a person's relationship patterns is "stroke economy." The listing of a person's stroke economy can be helpful.

Counselor: Let's do this. I want to list the significant people in your life.

Client: Do you mean the ones I like?

Counselor: Yes. But also the people that you interact with on a regular basis. The people who are in your life.

Client: My husband, my sister, my mom. I guess my boss and my co-worker. Oh, yes, my father-in-law.

Counselor: I'm going to list these; and as I do, I want you to rate them as a +++, ++, +, or a –, ––, –––. The pluses and minuses represent a continuum from very positive to very negative in regards to your interactions with them. This should help you to get a picture of your stroke economy. *(The counselor goes through the list and writes the responses on the board.)*

> Husband ––
>
> Sister + + +
>
> Mom –––
>
> Boss ––
>
> Co-worker –––
>
> Father-in-law –––

Client: No wonder I don't feel good. And what's sad is I talk to my sister only once a month or so.

Counselor: This is real important. It is hard to feel positive when you are around people whom you have negative interactions with.

Client: What do I do about this?

Counselor: That is what our counseling needs to be about. What changes can you make and are you willing to make to improve your stroke economy? Who can we add to the list? Who needs to be deleted?

Boxes

Clients, at times, feel boxed in either by their parents' rules, their boss's rules, their religious rules, or some other person's rules. One client that I saw had a very small, constrictive view of religion, so I drew a diagram of his religious box and what I thought God's religious box might be. (Actually in this case I asked a minister, who was a former student of mine, to co-counsel with me for a few sessions since my client said he wanted to discuss The Bible and religious issues.)

GOD'S VIEW OF RELIGION

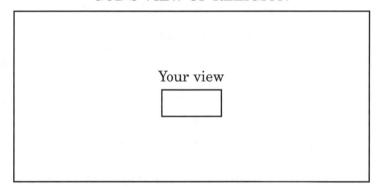

Counselor: Can you see how your very narrow view of religion has most of your behavior as a violation of God's desire for you?

Minister: God wants you to live an enjoyable life. It is okay to relax and rest.

Client: Not in my little box. Let's keep talking because I can see how I really have boxed myself in. I think God doesn't like the way I pray.

Minister: God does not have many rules about prayer.

Rational-Emotive Therapy

The basic premise of RET is that we tell ourselves irrational, self-defeating sentences (Walen, DiGiuseppe, and Wessler, 1980). The RET therapist helps the client to identify what she is telling herself and then tries to help the client dispute her negative self-talk. It is very effective to do this in writing so that the client can actually see what she is telling herself. For further elaboration of RET and how to use it, I suggest you read *A Practitioner's Guide to Rational-Emotive Therapy* by Walen et al. (1980).

Even if you are not familiar with RET or do not use it often, a good technique is to write out certain things that clients say so that they can see them.

Example 1

Counselor: Let me put up here what you are saying. *(Goes to the easel.)* You are saying, "My father drinks; therefore, I am a bad person." Look at that. Do you see anything wrong with that sentence?

Client: My dad should not drink? That's what is wrong!

Counselor: No, look at the sentence and tell me if you see something wrong with the logic.

Client: Uh, ...my dad's drinking has nothing to do with me as a person?

Counselor: That's right, but you have yourself believing that it does. Let's see what you could tell yourself about your dad's drinking.

Example 2

Client: ...I'm stupid. I'll never amount to anything.

Counselor: Let's list your grades here. You have an A in English, an A in history, an A in math, and a B in science; and you say you are stupid. I don't get it! That doesn't look like a stupid person to me.

       English ------- A

       History ------- A = STUPID ????

       Math --------- A

       Science ------ B

Client: Now that you have my grades written up there, I see that I am not stupid or I would not have made any A's.

Letters

Many clients are seen once a week or once every 2 weeks. In order to keep the client encouraged about the changes he is making, I have used a letter writing technique. That is, I have had the client bring to the session a self-addressed, stamped envelope with an encouraging letter that he has written to himself. Early in the week, I mail the letter so that he receives it about midway between the time we see each other again. Sometimes I may add a brief note to the letter, or the client may add to it before he gives it to me at the end of our session.

A variation of this can be for the therapist to send a brief note of encouragement during the week. Naturally this would be too time consuming to do for all clients, but there may be some clients that this would greatly benefit.

Written Homework

A counselor may want to give his client homework for a variety of reasons (Corey, 1991; Walen et al., 1980). He may want to keep the client thinking or heighten the client's awareness of her behavior, so he asks her to keep a list of the times she gets angry or to write a page on "what is a good daughter?" He may want to save time, so he asks the client to prepare something, such as an autobiography or a list of the pro's and con's of some decision. Listed below are some of the many written homework activities that you can ask a client to do.

Write a page on:
What makes one a worthwhile person?
What is a good mother?
What is a good son?
What do you owe your parents?
What is a man?
What is a woman?
What is my purpose in life?
What is fun for me and why?
How my childhood influences me now?

Keep a list of:
The things you worry about.
The times you feel scared.
The times you feel good.
The "shoulds" you tell yourself.
The times you fight.
Things you do that you like.
Things you do that you do not like.
Feelings you have during the week.

Write a letter to: (don't necessarily send it)
Yourself.
A part of yourself.
A parent.
A friend.
An ex-lover.
A person who is dead.
Keep a journal of thoughts, feelings, ideas, dreams.

The counselor usually would want to take some time to read what the client has written or allow her to discuss her written work during the session. The counselor may even want to keep what the client has written and then give it back the following week with some encouraging comments written by the counselor.

Transactional Analysis Drawings

In TA, the counselor talks of the person having three ego states, the Parent, the Adult, and the Child, which can be represented in the following diagrams (Campos & McCormick, 1985).

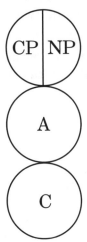

Very briefly described, the Critical Parent (CP) is the "shoulds" or critical part; the Nurturing Parent (NP) is the warm, supportive part of a person; the Adult (A) is the rational, thinking, computing part; and the Child (C) is either the fun part or the "not okay" part. I have decided not to describe TA in any detail, but rather to give a few examples that I think are helpful even if you are not very familiar with the theory. If you have no understanding of TA, then this section may be difficult for you to grasp. For a complete discussion of the ego states and the theory, please refer to one of the many good books on TA. Two that I suggest are *Born to Win* by James & Jongeward (1978) and *TA Today* by Stewart & Joines (1987).

A Dominating Part

Some clients have a part of themselves that dominates. Seeing this drawn out can be quite helpful.

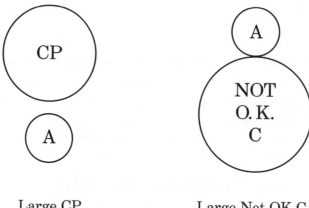

Large CP   Large Not OK C

Showing a client the size of the ego states of a significant other and the ego states of the client when the two interact can be beneficial.

Counselor: Let me show you what happens when you talk to your mom. She has a huge Critical Parent, and you have a huge Hurt, Angry Child. Here's how this would look.

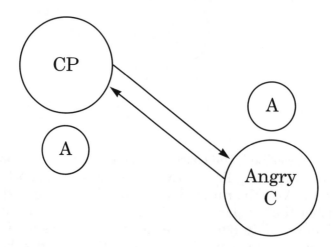

Client: No wonder we don't talk. How do I get her to her Adult?

Counselor: The first question is how do you get to your Adult. Let's focus on you first.

Communication Patterns

TA can be used to help clients understand their interactions with others. Communication patterns can be made visual by the use of TA drawings.

Counselor: Zack, let me show you in TA terms what happens when you get with your sister. You start in your Adult with a small Child. It would look like this.

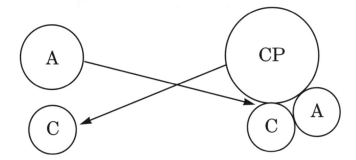

Then she starts to poke fun at you and says some cruel things, and your Child "swells"; and then all your communication is from your Child. What she is saying is "let's your Child and my Child fight," and you say, "okay." Let me draw this for you.

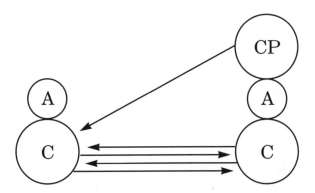

I could give many more examples, but my purpose is to show those of you who are not using TA some examples that may help you see how the drawings can be instrumental in helping a client understand himself and his interactions with others.

Egograms

An egogram is an excellent visual graph of a person's personality from a TA point of view (Dusay, 1980). The egogram is usually drawn using the five egostates. In the example below, the client has a large Critical Parent and a large Not Okay Child, which means that she is hard on herself and does not feel good about herself.

Counselor: I want us to draw a bar graph that represents your ego states. Let's take the critical parent first. Would it be very large?

Client: Yes, very large. *(The counselor and client draw the following egogram.)*

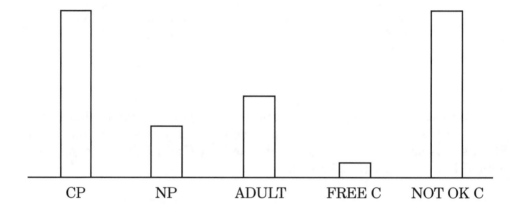

Counselor: As you look at your egogram, I think you can see where you need to do work.

Client: *(Looking at the drawing)* I have got to quit beating up on myself. Also, I have got to work on lowering the Not Okay Child.

Drama Triangle

In the TA literature, a triangle is sometimes used to illustrate the games that people are playing. The triangle is called the "drama triangle" because it describes the drama that often takes place when psychological games are being played (Stewart & Joines, 1987). In the example below, the counselor uses the drama triangle to help the client understand the fights she has with her husband.

Counselor: Let me draw something that I think will help you to see what is going on. This is called the drama triangle, with one point being the Persecutor, one point being the Victim, and one point being the Rescuer.

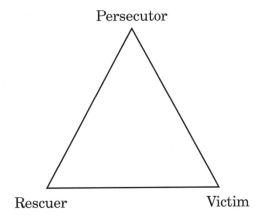

Persecutor

Rescuer   Victim

Counselor: When your husband calls and says he'll be home and then is over an hour late, you feel like the Victim and he's the Persecutor. *(Counselor stands at the easel and points to roles.)* Then when he comes home, you switch to Persecutor; and he feels like a Victim. Then he switches back and yells at you about your weight, and then you feel bad and start crying *(points to Victim)*. He then or later switches to Rescuer.

Client: Gosh, you are exactly right. We do that all the time, although sometimes I play Rescuer. How do we stop all this? *(Client walks to the drawing and moves her hand around, indicating the switching of roles.)*

The rest of the session would center on helping her not to play one of the three roles, and having the triangle there to refer to helps remind the client of what she needs to do.

Scripts

TA therapists help their clients understand their life scripts (Steiner, 1974). I often use a visual script concept to dramatize this for the client.

Counselor: It's like this. You wrote a script for yourself when you were about 10 years old. *(The counselor takes a sheet of paper and folds it in half and then writes on it, "Leah's Life Script.")* If you keep living out the script you wrote for yourself, with the help of your parents, teachers, and others, you will continue to do what you are doing. In order for you to be happy, you are going to need to do something with your script.

Client: What?

Counselor: What do you think?

Client: *(Staring at the script in the counselor's hands)* Yuk. I have got to do something. I can't stand the way I'm living.

Counselor: What about your script?

Client: I think I need to tear it up and write a new one.

Counselor: Are you sure? *(Hands the client the script)*

Client: *(Hesitates, and then tears it up.)* Gosh, I feel relieved or something. This is weird. I do see your point about my script.

Board of Directors

This drawing activity can be used in conjunction with the TA egostates, or it can be used alone. The drawing of one's "Board of Directors" can be a very powerful and meaningful activity. It is used to help clients see who influences them in the running of their lives.

Counselor: We've been talking about all these people you listen to when you go to decide something. What I want us to do is decide who is on your board of directors. *(Counselor draws board table with a number of chairs around it.)*

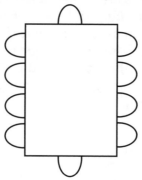

Counselor: Every one of us has an internal board of directors that we listen to when we decide things. Some have good boards, and some don't. Some have board members that have been on the board too long and no longer understand what the person is about, or they have their own agenda for the person. Some people have a board that has their addiction at the head; others have work as the head, and others have people that are no longer living on their board. In other words, your board consists of the powerful forces in your life. Who would be on your board?

Client: Can my husband be on the board?

Counselor: Sure, he may even head your board.

Client: Am I on my board?

Counselor: That's a good question? A person can be on her own board; in fact, she can head the board. However, in your case, I am not sure if you sit on the board or sit in a chair away from the board, just listening. *(The counselor writes the various names by the drawn seats.)*

Client: My mom is on the board, bigtime! She messes up every meeting *(client laughs but then gets serious)*.

There are many different ways to use this. The counselor can talk about firing some board members, adding some board members, and/or getting the client to be at the head.

If the client is familiar with TA, the counselor can suggest the client put different ego states on the board. Often, clients will put either their Critical Parent ego state or their Not Okay Child ego state as chairperson. Some of them do not put their Free Child on the board, which indicates that they don't have much fun in their lives.

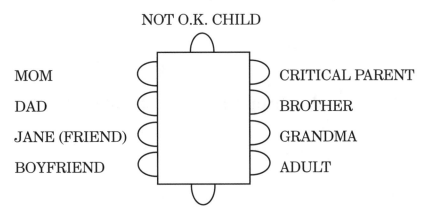

Counselor: What thoughts and feelings do you have as you look at this?

Client: No wonder my life is a mess. My Adult just sits in on the meetings but doesn't speak up, and my Free Child isn't even at the meetings. I have got to get in charge and get rid of my own Critical Parent and mom and dad. They do not belong on the board. This is our third session, and I can see now that counseling can help me. I wasn't sure before. This is such a good image for me. I'm going to copy this and take it home with me.

Boundaries

In the current work with co-dependency, the concept of boundaries is often discussed (Love, 1990; Mellody, 1989). By drawing boundary issues for clients, you provide a visual picture of what is going on.

Counselor: Mindy, you don't have yourself separate from your boyfriend or your roommate, so you often end up feeling hurt. Let me show you what you look like.

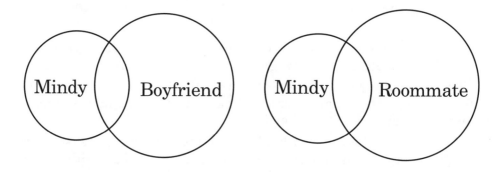

Counselor: How do you think these drawings should look?

Client: I guess with me separate from them. (*Counselor draws her as separate.*)

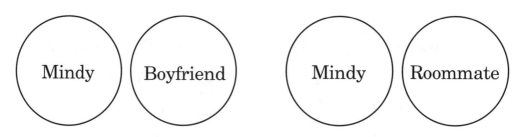

Client: All my life I've been told I get too attached. I think the circles help me to see what I've been doing all my life. You can change me?

Counselor: Well, no, I can't do that. I can work with you and help you to change you.

Family Boundaries

In family therapy the term, "enmeshment," is used to describe an over involvement with another person, usually a parent with a child, but it can be siblings or the marital couple (Love, 1990). I recently had a case where a 15-year-old girl chose to have an abortion against her parents' wishes, and the mom was devastated. Because of her enmeshment with the daughter, the mother felt that she herself had "murdered a child." I used the following drawing to help her to see that she was a separate person.

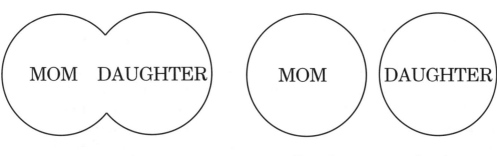

= Mom got an abortion   = Daughter got an abortion

The dialogue went something like this:

Counselor: There is a big difference in these two drawings. In the one on the left, it's like there is one person. This is how you are seeing this situation. It really is your daughter's situation; but if I can't get you to realize that you and Helen are two different people, it is going to be hard for you to feel better. Look at the drawings. *(Client looks.)* What are you seeing?

Client: This has been the worst week of my life. I cannot go on feeling this way, and I will if I can't see myself as separate from Helen. The picture on the right makes sense, but it is hard.

Counselor: If you can get there, though, you then may be able to be supportive of your daughter or at least not make her feel like she did a horrible thing.

Client: I know my attitude is not at all helpful to her. I think I can use the drawings to help me not feel so much pain. After all, she is her own person.

Counselor: You really are on the right track with this. Keep talking.

Another case I recently had involved a woman who felt responsible for her alcoholic sister. She was a few years older than her sister and had practically raised her due to her parents' drinking problems. Because her sister was not in any kind of recovery program, my client did not feel that she herself had the right to be happy. I drew her enmeshment and then drew a wall that was needed to establish separate boundaries.

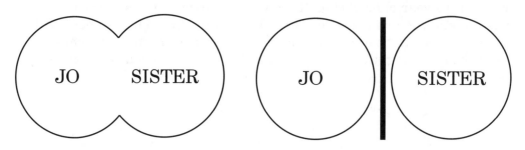

She said that seeing her relationship on paper was very helpful, and she took the drawings with her to remind her of what she needs to do.

There are many other drawings that I have done, depending on the presenting problem. I have drawn two paths, where one heads to a good life and the other heads to nowhere or to prison or to alcoholism. I have drawn a person trying to go somewhere and the many obstacles that are in the way. I have drawn a line that shows that getting better is not always straight ahead but rather some gains and losses.

Counselor: Getting better is not a straight line. The progress looks more like this:

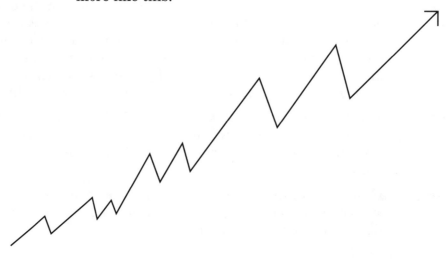

Client: I guess I never thought that I would have ups and downs. I was on such a roll there for a while.

Counselor: Often at the beginning, clients feel very good and then some rough times hit. What I am saying is that your feelings are normal.

Client: I think I'll take this drawing home with me.

6 Analogies and Fantasies

In this chapter, I discuss numerous analogies and fantasies that can be used to enhance counseling. The analogies (also called "metaphors" in the literature) are helpful because clients tend to remember them, and they can serve as a focusing point during the session(Haley, 1986: Meier, 1989; Young, 1992). The use of fantasy during a counseling session may provide a unique way to access information about how the client sees herself.

Analogies

Analogies are used to help the client gain better understanding of his problem (Hill, 1992). In this section, I describe many different analogies. As you read these examples, you will probably think of many other analogies that would be useful. Many times I use the ones described here, but often I will make up one to fit the client's specific situation. When using metaphors, you should pick one that the client can relate to. In other words, you may want to use sports analogies for those who are into sports, and you would not use a "dieting" metaphor for a person who is quite thin. In the examples presented in this chapter, the dialogue is abbreviated since my purpose is to present the general idea of how the analogy can be used.

Learning a New Language

When a client is struggling with putting into practice the changes that are discussed in counseling, I sometimes use the analogy of learning a language.

Counselor: I know this is new for you. It is like learning a new language. You have never thought this way, and it is going to take some time and practice. There is no way for you to automatically start thinking like this; but if you work at it, you will be able to do it. If you suddenly were told to stop thinking in English and start thinking in German, could you do it immediately?

Client: No, I don't know any German.

Counselor: However, if you study German and practice it daily, by the end of a year do you think you would know a lot of German?

Client: I would think so.

Counselor: Counseling is similar. Eventually, thinking this new way will become familiar and easy for you. You have been thinking one way all your life, and now you are discovering that there is another way to think about yourself and about life. It will take time to learn this new language–this new way of thinking.

Taking Lessons

Many clients come for counseling regularly but do not think about the session once it is over. They may even get frustrated because the counseling does not seem to be helping. The following analogy may be useful.

Counselor: Have you ever taken any kind of lessons, say tennis, piano, or anything?

Client: I took piano lessons for a while, but I never did get very good.

Counselor: Did you practice between lessons?

Client: The first year I did. That was when I did the best.

Counselor: That's exactly my point. Counseling is like taking lessons. You have to practice between sessions. What you do is come here, listen, and then leave; but you continue to act basically the same as you did before you came. I give you tasks to do such as reading or trying some different things, but each week you come back and say that you did not have time or that you forgot. For counseling to be helpful, you need to see it like your first year of piano lessons. There is the lesson, which is the counseling session; and there is the practicing, which is doing the different things we discuss.

Client: The comparison makes sense. I guess I was coming here thinking that you would "fix" me. I didn't realize that I needed to practice.

Counselor: What you do and think between sessions is equally as important as what we do here.

Dieting

I use a dieting analogy to point out how changing takes discipline. The metaphor of dieting can also be used when discussing how counseling takes patience.

Example 1

Counselor: It all boils down to discipline. It's like dieting. A person can have all the insight in the world about why he is fat; but to lose the weight, the person has to stop eating certain foods and pay attention to the amount that he eats. You are like the person who says, "I want to diet, but I also want to continue eating pizza and ice cream." If you want to stop feeling bad about yourself, you are going to have to find some positive people and activities. You can't continue doing what you are doing and feel better. The dieter has to change his eating habits. You have to change your living habits.

Client: The example is a good one. I often talk about losing weight, but only once did I truly diet. Then I lost weight. I guess you are saying the same is true with my problems. I talk about them, but I don't really do anything different. I do want to change the way I am feeling!

Counselor: Great. Let's talk about your new counseling diet.

Example 2

The counselor has been talking to the client about her impatience with counseling.

Counselor: Did you ever lose weight?

Client: Yes, 30 pounds.

Counselor: Did you do that in 2 or 3 weeks?

Client: No. It took me about 5 months.

Counselor: I don't think you realize that counseling is going to take some time. You don't just come here and get cured. It will take time, just like dieting. It also takes a conscious effort on your part, just like when you dieted. During that 5 months of dieting, you were aware of what you ate and probably how much you exercised. At first, I imagine it was hard; then it got easier and more familiar.

Client: That's right. I just never thought that counseling and dieting had much in common; but now that you mentioned it, it sure makes sense.

Skiing

This analogy is helpful for those clients who want their counseling to be easier and faster.

Client: I don't know if the counseling is worth it. It seems like it is going to take a long time; and many times when I am here, I don't feel comfortable.

Counselor: It's like learning to snow ski. Did you ever ski?

Client: Yes, what a tough thing to learn!

Counselor: That's right. I'll bet it was very awkward at first. *(Client nods.)* Just being in the boots was tough enough. And then it was hard to move around with the skis on. Then you had to negotiate getting on and off the lift.

Client: It was one of the most difficult things I have ever done. I thought I would never learn. But I did, and now I ski fairly well. I go skiing many times a year.

Counselor: My point is, you did not start out comfortably on the advanced slopes. You had to take it step by step. No one starts on the advanced slopes. Let's talk about how your learning to ski is similar to your learning new ways to think and act.

Driving a Standard Shift Car

This analogy is similar to the skiing one above in that it addresses the awkwardness of changing.

Counselor: Did you ever learn to drive a stick shift car?

Client: Yes, when I was in driver's education.

Counselor: Was it difficult?

Client: I sure thought so. It seemed like there was so much to think about, all at the same time.

Counselor: After getting used to it, what happened?

Client: It got easier, and then it became second nature. I don't even think about it now.

Counselor: The process is the same for counseling. Right now it is awkward, and you have to think about what you are doing and telling yourself because you are learning new ways of doing things. There seems to be a lot to learn and concentrate on, but if you stick with it, all of this will become second nature to you, just like driving.

Client: Well, I hope so. It sure does feel like driver's education. In some ways it is; only instead of a car, I am learning to drive myself in a safe, better manner.

Counselor: That's exactly right.

Remodeling Your House

Clients often feel as though counseling causes them to reconstruct or remodel their lives.

Counselor: Tony, the counseling you are doing is like a remodeling job on your house. You and I are taking a look at the foundation and all the rooms in your house. First, we worked on the foundation by helping you to better understand your childhood and what happened. We are now looking into all the rooms and how we can knock down some walls, change some things, make some rooms larger, and add some rooms. Construction takes time, some temporary disruptions, and some trust that things will be much better and more comfortable than before the remodeling.

Client: That's a good analogy. I actually did remodel my house a couple of years ago. I never knew there was so much involved. In fact, I got impatient and hurried some things, so they did not turn out exactly the way I wanted them to.

Counselor: Good point. Let's make sure you do not hurry this remodeling job. It is a very important job. This can help you be comfortable for a long time if you take your time and look at all that needs to be done.

Gardening

Comparing counseling with gardening can be a useful metaphor.

Counselor: Have you ever put in a garden?

Client: I do one each year. Some years I am more into it than other years. This year I have not been into it.

Counselor: Well, Nancy, counseling is a lot like gardening. First, the ground is prepared for the seeds; then some seeds are planted. The garden is weeded while the seeds are taking hold and starting to grow. Additional seeds are periodically planted to add to the garden, all while weeding is continued in order for the plants to grow and not be overrun by unwanted weeds. Many gardeners do not pay attention to the weeds, and all the growth eventually gets taken over by the weeds. The key is the weeding. Good gardeners enjoy the process of being out in the garden, weeding, and trying new and different things in the garden. Gardeners have to be patient and sometimes have to contend with the weather, bugs, and animals, but the gardener understands that all of those things are part of gardening.

Client: What a helpful way to get me to see what counseling is about. I am doing the counseling like I am doing my garden this year. I am not paying much attention. I don't weed, so no wonder I get overrun with weeds in my mind. It's like I am paying you to do the weeding, but that's only once a week, and a garden needs daily attention.

Correcting Something That You Learned

Counseling, at times, involves helping the client change something that he has thought all his life. Clients believe what their parents taught them even though the messages are not always true. This analogy about $2 + 2 = 5$ illustrates the problem.

Counselor: It's like when you were growing up your parents mistakenly taught you $2 + 2 = 5$. Now when you see $2 + 2$, you automatically think 5. What I am asking you to do is to learn the correct answer. That is, $2 + 2 = 4$. You are a good person and deserve to be here on this earth. Unfortunately, your parents taught you something else due to their own problems. Can you see that you were taught wrong?

Client: It's hard to stop believing something you have believed for so long.

Counselor: I know it is. But I want you to see that you simply were not taught correctly: $2 + 2 = 4$, not 5! Your parents should have taught you: "You are a good person! You deserve to be happy!"

Client: I think I am going to go home and write on a big sheet of paper, $2 + 2 = 4$! This helps.

Pack on Your Back

Clients often complain about the pressure they feel because they are doing too many things or taking care of too many different people.

Counselor: Manuel, it is like you have a backpack on your back with all these weights in it. You are so used to it being there, you hardly notice it. But it is there, and it weighs you down a lot. It is heavy. You started loading your pack when you were a kid by believing that it was your job to help your mom and your brothers. You still have those weights, and now you are continuing to add more by trying to help your wife and her family. Can you feel all that weight on your back?

Client: You bet! It is heavy, but I don't see any other way. I have to carry them.

Counselor: Interesting choice of words, because you do believe that you have to carry them. It's got to be heavy and full. How much can the backpack hold?

Client: Not much more. Heck, it's too full now. I want to take the pack off and rest, but I am afraid of what will happen.

Counselor: That is what I want to help you with.

Pot Bound

Certain clients will be living in situations that do not allow much growth and development. Usually the situation is a marriage, but it can be a small town, a job, or some other situation.

Counselor: Lindy, you are like a plant that has been put in a small pot. You have grown and will stay alive even in the small pot, but you will not grow to your full potential unless you find a bigger pot to grow in. You are "pot bound," and your roots are pressing up against the sides of the pot. You simply need a bigger and more nurturing environment. Given a different environment, I think you would grow and feel much freer, but in the pot you are in, you won't ever feel comfortable.

Client: How true. I do feel stifled. I never will be who I want to be unless I change pots. I didn't realize that counseling would cause me to take a look at all the things I am now looking at. I am not living in a nurturing environment.

Carpenter's Tools

Clients often use only a few ways to deal with their problems. One goal of counseling is to give the client more tools to use as she handles situations that arise.

Counselor: Maybe this analogy will help. You are like a carpenter who has only three tools in her tool box. You have a hammer, a screwdriver, and a saw. So one of those tools is used on any building problem you face.

Client: Are you saying that I am not using many tools in my life?

95

Counselor: What I am trying to show you is that there are many more psychological tools to choose from instead of crying, fighting, raging, or withdrawing. A good carpenter has many tools in her tool box and uses them in many different ways. She doesn't use a screwdriver on jobs that call for a chisel.

Client: You're saying that I need more tools?

Counselor: I am saying you will continue to have the same problems if you don't expand your psychological tool bag, such as being assertive and taking risks.

Erosion or Rust

To point out to clients that they need to stop what they are doing or there will be irreversible damage, I use the example of either erosion or rust.

Counselor: What do you know about the effects of erosion?

Client: Not too much. Erosion is the slow washing away of the soil?

Counselor: And if erosion goes on too long, what happens to the land?

Client: It can be ruined. I think that is the purpose of trees. Farmers and engineers can stop erosion by doing different things.

Counselor: That is right. And that is what I see happening. There is erosion going on in your family; and if it is not stopped, the damage will be permanent. Are you willing to do what it takes to stop the erosion?

Client: Maybe. There seems to be a lot of changes that will have to be made.

Counselor: Let's talk some more about the current damage and the damage that will happen if you do not decide to do something about your erosion problem. Stopping erosion can seem like a costly thing, but not to do it is far more costly.

Client: I actually saw a show on television recently that pointed out all the problems with erosion and how they can be corrected if the erosion is caught in time.

Counselor: The question is, do you want to stop the erosion in your life?

Boxing Match

This metaphor can be used in numerous ways. I use it when I am pointing out that the person needs to train for her battles with another person. I also use the analogy of boxing when I am trying to get a client to see how strong her Child ego state is.

Counselor: It's like a boxing match. Your Child ego state can beat you in a few rounds. Sometimes she knocks you out in the first round. I want to be your Adult's coach. I want to get you better prepared for the fights. I want you to learn how to keep your defenses up and learn how to block the punches. At first, our goal will be for you to go the distance and win the fight against your Child, even if it is a split decision. Eventually, I want you to get so strong that the Child won't even get in the ring with you.

Client: That would be great. Right now the Child is very strong and can throw a punch, and I am down for the count.

Counselor: I want you training at the counseling gym. We are going to get you in shape and so prepared that the Child cannot knock you down!

Client: That child is strong! Let's get started. I want to be champ!

Tennis

A tennis metaphor can be used for describing how a person does not have to play psychological games. I also use a tennis analogy when I want to talk about being ready and alert.

Example 1: Games

Counselor: People cannot make you play games with them. They may make you stand on the tennis court. But if they hit the ball to you and you just stand there, no game will be played. It is always your choice whether to play games with people.

Client: Are you saying that no matter what he does, I do not have to play his games?

Counselor: That's right. Only you can swing your racket.

Client: I have always felt he made me play. I am going to use this example to remind myself that I am in charge of whether I play his games. Thanks.

Example 2: Readiness

Counselor: Do you play tennis or have you ever watched tennis on television?

Client: I play some.

Counselor: When your opponent is about to serve, what do you do?

Client: I get ready.

Counselor: That's right. You are ready for a serve to either your forehand or backhand. Your feet are ready to move.

Client: That's right.

Counselor: What would happen if you did not get yourself ready?

Client: I'd miss most of the serves.

Counselor: That is what I am trying to do for you in counseling. I am trying to get you ready!

Client: I see. This is making more sense. You are trying to prepare me for anything that comes up. If I am prepared and ready, then no matter what comes up, I should be able to handle it.

Pilot Light

Clients will often discuss their indecision about wanting out of their "dead" marriage. Some clients will be struggling with whether they should keep trying in the marriage. On numerous occasions, I have used an analogy pertaining to the pilot light on the stove to help them think about their relationship.

Counselor: Let me help you look at your situation by using an analogy. Do you have a gas stove?

Client: Yes.

Counselor: On the stove, is there a pilot light?

Client: Yes.

Counselor: If the pilot is out and you turn the oven on, will you get a flame?

Client: No. Not if the pilot light is out. You have to have a pilot light. If it is out, all you are doing is turning on the gas. It is actually dangerous.

Counselor: In your marriage, is the pilot light out?

Client: Good question... *(In a sad, but confident voice)* It is out for me. I don't feel any romantic feelings.

Cheerleader Model

One way to offer a positive image regarding marriage and family living is to use the example of cheerleaders. This is probably my most favorite one; and, therefore, I teach it to all my clients and in all my classes and workshops.

Counselor: I want to discuss your marriage in terms of what I call the cheerleader model. If a team is losing a game 40 to 0, what will the fans most likely be doing?

Client: Many will be leaving. Many will be booing probably.

Counselor: That's right. Now, what will the cheerleaders be doing.

Client: The cheerleaders, well, uh, they will still be cheering.

Counselor: That's right! Cheerleaders never boo their team. They always cheer for the players. Now, let's turn to your marriage. Do you feel your husband cheers for you?

Client: No. Well, sometimes, but not very often.

Counselor: That's what I have gathered from what you have said. In fact, he boos you more than he cheers for you .

Client: But he could cheer for me, couldn't he?

Counselor: Sure, but he doesn't! You have tried to get him to be your cheerleader, and he doesn't seem to want to do that. I think you need to realize that as long as you stay married to him, you probably are not going to have a cheerleader.

Client: But I want one, and I do believe that marriage should be a cheerleading kind of thing.

Counselor: I agree. But you are not married to a person who believes in that model.

Hot Air Balloon

I have used a hot air balloon analogy in many different ways. I have often used it when I was trying to get clients to better understand why they were not getting anywhere with their counseling.

Counselor: I think I have an analogy that may help you. It's like you are in a hot air balloon, trying to take off; but in your basket are all these weighted bags, some weighing as much as 500 pounds. You try and try to lift off, but the weight causes you to not get off the ground. You look at the weights and understand that you need to throw some bags over the side, but you can't decide which ones, so you go nowhere. You are so afraid of throwing them over the side; and also you are somewhat afraid of taking off, even though you really do want to.

Client: Boy, that's a great analogy. As you were talking, I could see myself standing there, looking at the weights!

Counselor: You will never get to soar, unless you have the courage to let go of some things.

Movie

There are many ways to use the metaphor of movies with clients. The one that I use the most deals with the main characters, the producer, the director, and the quality of the movie.

Counselor: Let's look at your life as if it were a movie... Who is the director and producer of the movie?

Client: It sure isn't me! Now it is my mother and my wife.

Counselor: That's right. Do you want to become the producer and director?

Client: I sure do. I don't like the way the movie flows. It's boring and very repetitious.

Counselor: How do you feel about the characters in the movie? Would you want to change any of them?

Client: I think I would. Many of the major characters would only have small parts, maybe not even be in the movie.

Counselor: You seem to grasp that your movie isn't an academy award winner.

Client: To be honest, it's a box office flop.

Counselor: How do you feel about that?

Client: I don't want it to be a flop. I see I have to take charge and become the producer and director.

Fantasies

When a counselor asks the client to imagine something, she is using the technique of fantasy. Fantasy can be very helpful, because clients may discover material that they have been repressing (Egan, 1990; Okun, 1992; Polster & Polster, 1973). Fantasy can be used during the session when the client says something like, "I don't really have anything to talk about today." Fantasy also can be used as part of the counseling process to help the client delve further into something that is being discussed. Examples are given of both.

You may be familiar with the use of fantasy if you studied group counseling, since fantasies are one kind of exercise that group leaders utilize (Corey, 1990; Gladding, 1991). Some group fantasies are mentioned here because they also can be used with individuals. The first two fantasies I discuss here are similar to the last two analogies mentioned in the first section of this chapter.

Hot Air Balloon Fantasy

Counselor: I want you to close your eyes and imagine yourself in a hot air balloon, trying to lift off; but you can't due to the extra bags of weight... Look at those bags and figure out what they represent and how much they weigh... What do you see?

Client: My job, my religion, and my marriage. They are my big weights. I have some small ones, too. A couple of them I had never thought about, but I saw some small bags. Actually the bags aren't so small. They are my age and my feelings about my ex-wife.

Movie Fantasy

Counselor: *(Speaking softly and slowly)* I want you to close your eyes and imagine that you are at a movie theater and you have just settled into your seat. The lights dim, and the title of the movie comes across the screen: "The Life of Sam Callen" *(the client's name)*. How does it feel knowing that a movie of your life is being shown in the theater?... The next sequence on the screen is the list of the producer and director and the main characters. Look at that list. How do you feel as the names come on the screen?... The movie begins. As you watch the film, what is your reaction to the main character and the different scenes that appear? ... Take some time and watch the movie... As you leave the theater, how are you feeling?... Listen to what people are saying as they leave the theater. What do you hear?

You can stop during the fantasy and talk about each part, or you can go through the entire fantasy and then discuss the various questions and reactions. I would suggest you try both ways and see which one works best for you. Remember, that with this fantasy, as with any fantasy, your voice pattern and tone are very important. You will want to make sure that you don't speak too fast and you use a voice that tends to get the client to relax, think, and/or feel.

Five-Year Follow-Up

Counselor: I want you to try something that may help you to get some insights. Close your eyes and get comfortable... It is 5 years from now... I want you to imagine that you just got the mail and you are opening a letter from me. I am asking you to comment on your life, 5 years after therapy. There is a series of questions about where you are living... what job you are doing... what your living situation is *(married, divorced, single, children?)*... how you are feeling about how your life is going... I want you to think about how you are going to answer the questions about your life 5 years from now...

Client: There's a lot there. I had myself living in Florida, and my wife was not there. I was alone. I wonder what that means?

Counselor: Do you want to explore that now or tell your reactions to the entire fantasy?

Client: Let's first go through the different questions.

Animal Fantasy

This fantasy can be used to get the client to talk about herself in a different way (Stevens, 1971). Almost always, the comments by the client about the animal are actually comments about how she would like to be.

Counselor: I'd like to try something different. If you could be any animal in the world, what animal would you like to be? Think about it for a minute... Does one come to mind?

Client: Yes. I would like to be a cat.

Counselor: Why a cat?

Client: They are mostly independent, but they do depend somewhat on their owners. Also, they are cared for and can get petted usually when they want to be. They also can choose to ignore what is happening around them.

Counselor: Let's take a look at your life. What insights can you get from your description of being a cat?

Client: I don't feel independent, and I sure want to.

Counselor: What else? This fantasy really is about you and not about cats.

Client: I'd like to be able to ignore things at times. In fact, that is a big problem of mine.

In the above example, the client has disclosed some important things about herself, and the counselor can use the rest of the session to discuss the concerns that came up as a result of the fantasy. Some counselors make the mistake of talking about the animal rather than understanding that the animal fantasy serves as a projection of how clients want to be or how they see themselves.

Pick an Object in the Room

This fantasy is similar to the animal fantasy above, but instead of picking an animal, you have the client look around and pick an object in the room (Stevens, 1971).

Counselor: We seem to be bogged down. Let's try something that may get us going in some new directions. I want you to look around the room and pick an object that you are going to become. Pick any object, such as the door, the light, the window, whatever... Do you have one?

Client: Yes, the file drawer.

Counselor: Good. *(Softening his voice)* Now, what I want you to do is to imagine that you are the file drawer. What is life like as a file drawer?... How does it feel being a file drawer?... Now I want you to tell me about being a file drawer, but do it in first person, present tense. Start with, "I'm a file drawer and here's what life is like. I..."

Client: I saw the file drawer.

Counselor: *(Cutting off the client, using a kind voice)* No, talk as if you are the file drawer. I'm a file drawer. Do you understand?

Client: I understand. I am a file drawer. I keep a lot inside of me. I sometimes feel very important, and sometimes I feel meaningless and forgotten. I have some secrets tucked away in the back that I hope no one finds. I feel like I would like to be cleaned out, but so far no one has done that.

Counselor: Very interesting. Sandy, what do you think all of that means? Instead of thinking as a file drawer, think of yourself. How do you feel meaningless and forgotten? Probably the bigger question is "What secrets do you have that you are afraid to share?" Let's talk about meaningless first, and then see if you are comfortable talking about the secrets.

Other objects can be used for this kind of fantasy, as well. Recently, I received a letter from a former participant in one of my workshops who shared how he used an empty Coke can. Stevens (1971) described how he uses a rosebush and a motorcycle as fantasies for group members.

Visit to the Wise Person

Stevens (1971) discussed this fantasy. You can vary the fantasy to fit the client, but basically it deals with a person going to visit a wise person and asking for answers. In the example below, the client is asked to find out the meaning to life since she has been struggling with changes in her own life.

Counselor: We have been discussing many different choices and changes. You have sought advice from different people and their answers clash. Let's try something different. I want you to close your eyes and relax... *(Speaking slowly)* I want you to imagine that it is a Saturday, and you are up early and are preparing to go on a journey to see this wise person who lives in the mountains. You have heard that this person can give you the answers to the questions you have been asking. As you prepare to go, you have many different feelings about going to see this person... You even think about not going, but you decide you are ready to find out the answers... You were told that you can come alone or with one other person... You were told that it is usually best to come alone or with someone who truly understands you... You drive to the spot where you are to park, and you start the hike up the mountain to find the wise person... As you get near where you are to meet this person, you are trying to get clear as to what questions you are going to ask. You know that you are allowed only three questions... Now you are there. How are you feeling?... The wise person greets you and asks you to sit down. The wise person then asks for your questions... *(The counselor speaks even softer)* You will want to get in touch with the different thoughts and feelings you are having as the wise person responds... Now you are ready to start down the mountain. You are deep in thought as you descend... As the car comes into view, you decide to sit and think for a few more minutes. You know this has been a valuable experience... I'd like you now to open your eyes and tell what you experienced.

Client: Whew!!! What a powerful experience. It's going to take me a moment to collect my thoughts.

This fantasy can be very meaningful if conducted properly. You will want to make sure that you talk in a soft, slow manner and that you allow enough time for the person to imagine whatever it is that you are asking him to do.

Using fantasies is a powerful way to help your clients. In addition to those discussed here, you can make up others that relate to your particular clients.

7 Using Creative Techniques in Groups

Many of the creative techniques mentioned in the previous chapters also can be used in group situations. This chapter is written for those leaders who use exercises in their groups and for those leaders who take an active role when leading a therapy group.

Before describing the use of creative techniques in groups, I want to briefly comment on my view of group leadership. I believe that in most counseling settings, such as schools, mental health centers, rehabilitation centers, and hospitals, groups need to be conducted by a leader who plans and facilitates the group process. The leader is active and responsible for assuring that the group is meaningful and productive.

In this chapter, I describe exercises but do not discuss processing skills. If you are interested in learning more about how to conduct and process exercises or about group counseling in general, I would suggest you read *Group Counseling: Strategies and Skills* by Jacobs, Harvill, and Masson (1988) or any of the following from the reference list in the back of this book: Corey (1990), Gladding (1991), or Trotzer (1989).

If you have little or no experience with this kind of group leadership, you may find this chapter to be somewhat frustrating because you will want to know more about what to do once you have used the creative technique. If so, please see Jacobs et al. (1988) or other group books that are specifically about how to lead groups.

Creative Techniques as Exercises

By using creative techniques, a group leader can add to her list of exercises to be used when conducting a group. I have divided this section into the same categories as Chapters 2 through 6: props, chairs, movement, writing and drawing, and analogies and fantasies. Many of these exercises are simple and quick, and yet they can be very powerful and help group members focus on their issues.

Props

Cups

There are many ways in which cups can be used as a group exercise. The leader would need to have a styrofoam cup for each member.

Example 1

Leader: We have been talking in general about self-worth and how we often don't feel good about ourselves. I want to do an exercise with you that I think can take our discussion to a deeper, more personal level. I want each of you to hold up the cup I gave you. I want you to think of the cup as your "worth," and now I want you to think of what leaks you have in your worth cup. As you think of the leaks, take your pencil and punch holes in your cup. Leaks can be anything, such as not feeling smart enough, believing that your dad doesn't like you, not being pretty enough... Everybody done? *(Members nod.)* Let's get some comments. Who wants to share your worth cup?

Example 2

This can be conducted with one cup or with each person having a cup and the leader collecting the cups.

Leader: We have been talking about self-worth, and it has become obvious to me that most of you give your worth to others, especially your dating partner and your parents. It's like this cup represents your worth. *(Leader slowly rises and stands in his chair)* And you turn your worth over to someone, and they can smash you *(all eyes are on the leader who is squeezing the cup)*. Who do you give your worth to?... What are you feeling as you see your worth being squeezed?

Rubber Bands

Rubber bands can be used to represent tension between members in a group, couples in a couples group, or within one member.

Leader: There seems to be much tension in the group; and in order for this group to be productive, we have to reduce the tension. I have five hefty rubber bands that we are going to use to represent the tension, and then we are going to talk about ways to reduce the tension. There is one absolute rule–you cannot intentionally let go of the rubber band and hurt someone. If you do that, I will ask you to leave the group. I think I know where there is tension, but I am going to ask any of you to point out tension between people in the group.

Member: I think there is a lot of tension between Horace and Jim. *(Other members nod.)*

Leader: I agree. Horace, I want you to move next to Jim. *(He does this.)* Now each of you take an end of the rubber band and stretch it until it nearly breaks. Now you sit there and experience that tension while we see if there are other tension spots.

The leader could process this in many different ways, depending on the amount of tension, the kind of group, and the make up of the members. This creative technique has many possibilities.

Video Tapes

Leader: Today I want us to discuss how each of you feel about your life and if you want to change your life. I want to start with an exercise that should get you to think. *(Pause)* In my hands I have three video tapes *(two tapes look the same, and the other looks different)*. The one in my left hand is the tape of the last 2 years of your life. In the other hand are two blank tapes that can be used to record the next 2 years. Notice that one blank tape looks the same as the other tape. Also notice that the third tape looks different. Either one can be used for the next 2 years. I am going to set the tapes down on the floor, and I want you to look at them and think if you want to make the same tape for the next 2 years or make a different tape. *(Members stare at the different tapes. Many look deep in thought)*...

Debbie: I don't want to make the same tape! *(Others nod.)*

Leader: Debbie, what do you need to do to make sure you don't? Let me ask others of you. What does Debbie need to do in order to make her life different than the last 2 years?

Shelly: She needs to stop using drugs.

Joan: She needs to probably not be in that crazy job with those weird people.

These are just some examples of how props can be used as an exercise in group. You may want to review the Props chapter in this book for additional ideas or think of other props that can be used in groups you are leading.

Chairs

An empty chair can be used to create powerful exercises in a group (Gladding, 1991). A small, child's chair can also be used very effectively.

Chair in the Middle

Groups are usually led with the members sitting in a circle. In this example, the leader places an empty chair in the middle of the circle and has the members imagine that someone with whom they are angry is sitting in the chair.

Leader: Today we are going to discuss anger. To get you focused, I want each of you to think of someone you are currently angry with or someone you recently have been angry with and imagine that they are sitting in this chair *(in the center of the group)*... Everyone have someone? *(All nod.)* I would like you to briefly state who this person is to you. You might say "mother," "friend," "boss," "lover," or anyone else. Doug, you look ready.

Doug: Mom

Chris: Girlfriend

Dale: Dad

Rick: Brother

Sharon: Dad

Leader: Who is willing to share what you are angry about?

The leader can do many different things at this point, depending on how she wants to approach the subject. She can teach the RET idea of anger, which is that it is your thoughts that cause the anger and not the person in the chair. After teaching the theory, she could have different dialogues take place between members and the person they have in the chair and then discuss the imagined or role-played interaction from a RET framework.

The leader could also get different people to discuss their anger with the person in the chair and then have members comment in helpful ways. My main point is not so much how you approach the topic of anger in your groups, but rather to show how the empty chair can be helpful in generating energy for the topic. Also, members can be easily brought back to the topic by making reference to the chair in the center.

Standing on the Chair

A very simple exercise can be done with the leader standing on an empty chair.

Leader: From what many of you have said, there are people to whom you do not feel equal. I think it would be good to look at this further. Let me get you started. *(Leader gets up and stands in a chair. Members look up at him.)* Who do you have up here? Some of you have more than one person. Think about it. Who is up here?...

The leader could get members to share who they have standing on the chair. The leader could focus on different individuals and help them see that they don't have to put others up there. How you use this exercise will depend mostly on your group leadership style and the purpose of the group.

Small Chair

In Chapter 2, I gave examples of how a child's chair can be helpful in individual counseling. The same is true for group counseling. Many of the co-dependent groups and the ACOA groups focus on healing the wounded child. The chair can be used as a visual representation of the wounded child. In groups where TA is being used, the Child ego state can be symbolized by the small chair.

Example 1

Leader: I want you to look at this child's chair. (*All look at the chair. The leader speaks in a quiet, soothing voice.*) I want you to imagine that you are sitting there. Think of what you would liked to have heard from your parents or others that were involved in your upbringing.

To process this activity, the leader could have the members share any thoughts or feelings. Also, she could focus on any member who wants to work on the unresolved feelings. She could have different people go sit in the chair and hear positive things. The options are numerous.

Example 2

Leader: Many of you slide into your Child ego state when you are in certain situations. I want you to imagine sliding out of your Adult, which is the chair you are in and sliding into this chair (*a small chair that the leader has placed in the center of the group*). When do you do this?... Why do you do this?... Any comments or thoughts about this?

Tanya: I could feel myself sliding as I imagined myself talking to my father.

Susan: I go to my Child when I am with my boyfriend. How do I learn not to slide into that chair? I have been doing that ever since I started dating.

Leader: Getting in touch with how you slide into your Child and how not to do that is what I want us to focus on this week and perhaps for the next few weeks.

Movement

There are many excellent movement exercises that can be used to focus and energize groups. By movement, I mean the members get up and move around. Movement exercises are extremely valuable because the members are involved in doing something. Active, experiential learning usually generates group interest and energy.

I do not describe here some of the more common movement exercises, such as the blind trust walk or family sculpture, but rather concentrate on some movement exercises that are not so common.

Values Continuum

In this exercise, the members are asked to stand up, move to the center of the room, and line up in a straight line. The leader then designates one side of the room as a point of view and the other side as the opposite point of view. In the example below, the leader uses one wall as "winner" and one wall as "loser." There are countless value opposites that can also be used. For example, some leaders have used "risk taker/play it very safe," "spender/saver," or "happy/unhappy."

Leader: I want to do an exercise that should generate some discussion. I want you to stand up and line up behind Joe. *(The leader places Joe in the front of the group and in the center of the room. The members then line up behind Joe.)* In a minute, I am going to ask you to position yourself somewhere between the two walls. One wall will represent winner, and one wall will represent loser. I want you to think about how you feel about yourself. If you feel totally like a winner, then you will move all the way over to the wall on my right. If you feel totally like a loser, you will move to the wall on my left. Now on the count of 3 you will move. Ready. 1... 2... 3.

After the members move, the leader can get them to comment on their choices. The leader can encourage members to comment on whether they have always felt the way they do now or whether they have changed. Having everyone position themselves tends to generate more discussion than simply asking members to comment on their feelings about being a winner or loser.

Sculpt How You Feel About Group

Some groups will consist of members who do not want to be in the group or who do not feel comfortable being in the group. If you are ever the leader of such a group, you may decide to focus on the members' feelings about being in the group. One creative way to do this is through the movement exercise described below. This exercise works best if you have some members who feel reasonably positive about being in the group.

Leader: I think it would be good to talk about people's different feelings about being in this group. Here's what I would like you to do. Everyone stand up and make a large circle. *(Members do this.)* In a minute I am going to ask you to sculpt how you feel about the group. What I mean is that if you feel really into the group, you will move to the center and have your arms open to indicate your readiness. If you are approaching the group with openness but caution, you may want to put one foot forward and your arms partly open. *(The leader demonstrates this.)* If, on the other hand, you feel very turned off, you would probably turn around and fold your arms, indicating your dislike for being here. Everybody understand? Use your arms and movement either toward or away from the center of the group.

Members will usually position themselves in many different ways, and then either the leader or other members can comment or ask questions about the various positions. This usually proves to be a very interesting exercise if the timing is right.

Goals

For certain kinds of groups, members establish their personal goals during the early sessions and then work to accomplish those goals throughout the life of the group. This exercise can be used to help members see their progress and to encourage them to take additional steps.

Leader: Lately, I have felt that many of you have stalled in your movement toward accomplishing the goals that you set for yourself. I'd like to do this exercise that may help you. Everyone stand and line up next to each other near the wall. *(They do this.)* Where you are standing is where you started when we began this group. In a minute, I am going to ask you to move forward as much as you feel you have come in regards to your goals. If where I am standing is reaching your goals *(leader is about 8 feet in front of them)*, position yourself somewhere between where you are standing and me. If you feel you have made some progress, move forward to a position that represents your progress. If you feel like you have gone backwards, you can step back. Everyone understand? *(All nod.)*

After they position themselves, the leader can get members to comment about themselves or about other members. The leader can have members talk about how they are holding themselves back. There are many options. After some discussion, the leader may continue with the following:

Leader: I want each of you to take one step forward. I want you to think of what that step would be in regards to what you could do here in group today that would be a step towards reaching your goal. *(The members do this and are obviously thinking.)*... Anyone want to comment?

The next exercise can be very powerful if it is conducted properly. It deals with members having to struggle to reach their goals.

Leader: We are going to do an exercise that can allow you to experience some of the struggles you are going to have in trying to reach your goals. I want everyone to stand up. I want you to make two lines, about 4 feet apart. I want you to face the person across from you. *(They line up, three on* *one side and four on the other.)* Let me get a volunteer to go first, and then I will explain what we are going to do.

Tina: I'll do it even though I don't know what I'm volunteering for. Will it hurt?

Leader: No, but it should make you think. Tina, you come stand here at the beginning of the line, looking down the path you need to travel to reach your goal. At the other end is reaching your goals; and as you move down the path toward your goals, you will meet resistance. In other words, you will walk between the people; and they will offer resistance by pulling on you, blocking you, etc.

Note: If the members know each other well, they will know about how much resistance to create. For instance, in a long-term treatment center for adolescents, everyone would know each other and could probably represent different people or things (drugs, sex) that may keep the member from reaching her goal. In groups where the members do not know each other very well, the leader can ask the member to suggest the amount of resistance. Realize that there are many different ways that you can set this up and have it be effective. I have done this with people who just met each other, and it worked well. It is not important that the members in the line know what the goals are. The person going through the line will know.

Leader: Tina, how much resistance do you anticipate?

Tina: Lots at the beginning and then it should not be too bad.

Leader: Those at the beginning, don't make it too easy for Tina. You'll use your arms and body to symbolize the resistance. Also, though, don't make it impossible. Then as she gets to the middle, show some resistance but not too much. Tina, you ready?

Usually the best way to do this is to have everyone go through the experience of going down the path and then discuss their feelings and reactions.

Parents' Chat

This exercise can be helpful in getting members to take a look at how their parents feel about them (Stevens, 1971). Often the exercise precipitates a variety of reactions, all centering around parents.

Leader: I want to get you to do something a little different. What I am going to do is ask you to become one of your parents or a person who raised you. The person does not have to be living right now. What you are going to do is meet with two others, and the three of you are going to have a parents' chat about your children. You will not be yourself, but you will be one of your parents, and you will talk about your son or daughter. For example, Marty what is your father's name?

Marty: Joe.

Leader: When you introduce yourself, if you decide to be your father, you would say: "I'm Joe, and I have a son named Marty. I also have a daughter named Sara." *(Marty has talked about his sister in the group.)* You would mainly focus on Marty and how your Dad feels about him. Take a minute and think of who you want to be and what you want to say as that person...

Since there are nine members, number off 1, 2, 3. *(They number off.)* The 1's get together, the 2's, and the 3's.

The leader would let the people talk among themselves for 5 to 10 minutes and then bring the group back together for discussion. Members usually find this a very helpful and interesting exercise.

Feedback Lines

There are numerous useful feedback exercises. For example, feedback lines can generate much energy and interest because every member is active. You will want to be careful to use this only in situations where members are able and ready to participate in such an exercise.

Leader: For the next few minutes, we are going to do a feedback exercise. I want everyone to stand. Now I am going to ask for someone to volunteer to go first. This person is going to line up members of the group according to how he or she sees members working in the group. Who wants to volunteer?...

Roy: I guess I will.

Leader: What I want you to do is put the person you think is working the hardest at the front and then place the other people behind that person in the order that you see them working in this group. When you are done, I want you to step in where you feel you are. Any questions?

Roy: No, I think I got it.

The leader would have each person position the rest of the group. Then much discussion would take place about the different perceptions.

In the example above, the members were positioned according to their effort in the group. There are other reference points for the feedback, such as a recovery group using "those people you think are going to stay in recovery and those you think are going to relapse." You can have members line people up according to "those you trust the most to those you trust the least" or "those you feel most comfortable with to those you feel least comfortable with."

I include these feedback exercises because some of you will work in situations where they can be very valuable. If you use them, however, you must be prepared to deal with the reactions and emotions generated.

Writing and Drawing

Written exercises are very valuable for a group leader (Corey, Corey, Callanan, & Russel, 1988; Gladding, 1991; Jacobs et al., 1988). Members tend to be more involved if they have to write something. Written exercises can be helpful in drawing people out because the leader can ask the member to read what she has written. Most members don't feel on the spot if they have something written down. Written exercises include sentence completion, list making, or question answering.

Another way that writing is used effectively in some groups is when the leader asks the group to generate some list that he writes on the blackboard or wipe board. Topics could be "characteristics of a friend," "ways to find a job," or "problems you may have if you use drugs." If it is an interesting and relevant topic, members tend to get involved and focused.

Sentence Completion

Sentence completions are one of the most helpful tools to have in your group leader's tool box (Jacobs et al., 1988). For many first group sessions or for a group that is only going to meet once, a sentence completion consisting of three to five incomplete sentences can be an excellent way to get members talking.

Below are some examples of sentences to use in a first group:

1. In a new group, I feel _____

2. When people first meet me, they _____

3. In a new group, I am most afraid that _____

4. I feel annoyed when the leader _____

5. When people remain silent, I feel _____

The leader would ask the members to complete the sentences and then discuss them one at a time.

For other topics, the leader can create a short sentence completion. For instance, if you were leading a group on drugs, you could use the following:

1. I like drugs because _____

2. I dislike drugs because _____

3. My biggest fear about drugs is _____

4. I do not think that I have a problem with drugs because ____

_____

The sentence completion exercise is an excellent way to focus group members on topics that you want them to discuss.

Egograms and Board of Directors

In Chapter 5, I discussed two useful drawing activities, egograms and board of directors, that can be utilized in a group setting. To use these, you would have each member draw his board of directors (or his egogram), and then you would discuss them. Since both of these exercises generate much energy, when the members finish their drawings, I often will have them talk in two's or three's first before bringing the group together as a whole. This is to insure that everyone gets to talk about her drawing even if it is not in the large group.

Another way to use these drawings would be to have one person each week talk about his drawing. That is, one segment of group each week would allow 10 to 20 minutes for a person to present and discuss his egogram or board of directors.

Fantasies

In Chapter 6, I discussed how fantasies can be used with individual clients. I described the animal, the object in the room, the movie, the hot air balloon, and the wise person fantasies. All of these can serve as excellent group exercises. Members are usually very interested in hearing other members' fantasies (Gladding, 1991, Kotler, 1983, Stevens, 1971). Of the many different kinds of exercises that I use in groups, I have found fantasy exercises to be among the most productive.

One fantasy exercise that I use, but have not yet mentioned is the Common Object fantasy. In the example below, I use a briefcase as the common object. Almost any object will work just as well.

Leader: I want to do an exercise that members usually find very interesting. We are going to do a fantasy exercise, focusing on this briefcase. I want you to look at this briefcase that I have here. *(Leader slows voice and speaks softer.)* I want you to imagine that you are this briefcase… What is your life like as a briefcase?… How does it feel being a briefcase?… Take a minute and think about your life as a briefcase… Okay. Who wants to tell about being a briefcase? I'd like you to talk in first person, present tense. That is, say, "I am a briefcase. Here's how I feel…"

Mike: I'll go first. I am a briefcase, and I get banged around a lot. I think I am important, but no one seems to really appreciate me. I am even forgotten sometimes.

Eric: I'll go next. I am a briefcase. I get to travel to important places. I have a lot of valuable things inside and am helpful to my owner. It is exciting being in those important meetings and going to so many different places.

The leader usually lets each member tell his or her fantasy, and then members discuss their responses. The skilled leader guides the discussion so the members focus on their own lives rather than the life of a briefcase since their fantasies are usually a projection of how they see themselves.

Rounds

Since some group counselors are not familiar with the use of rounds, I want to include a brief section on this most useful exercise.

A round is an activity in which every member is asked to respond to some stimulus posed by the leader. The value of rounds cannot be overemphasized–there is no group skill, technique, or exercise mentioned in this book that is more valuable than the use of rounds. In tasks, education, and discussion groups, rounds are extremely helpful in gathering information and involving members. In support and therapy groups, rounds can serve a variety of therapeutic functions (Jacobs et al., 1988).

Rounds are a way to get members to share (Corey, 1990; Gladding, 1991). A round can be conducted quickly by asking for a designated word, number, or short phrase. The comment round takes a little more time. The value of the round lies in the fact that everyone shares, giving the leader some idea of what the members are thinking and/or feeling. For an in-depth discussion of rounds and how they can be used, see Jacobs et al. (1988). Below are some examples of rounds:

Example 1

The leader is about to begin the third session. She senses that the members are restless and wants to get them focused on group, so she uses a "here/not here" round.

Leader:	Let's start... I'd like get started by having you say either "here," "getting here," or "not here" regarding if you are ready to get started and are focused on group.
Donna:	Here.
Karen:	Getting here.
Linda:	Here.
Tony:	Not here.
Carl:	Getting here.
Dan:	Not here.
Leader:	What will it take to get you here? Do those of you who said "not here" or "getting here" want to comment?

In the next example, the leader uses a "yes/no" round to get an idea of who wants to bring up some issue in group. This is an excellent exercise to do near the beginning of the session in that it helps the leader locate the energy in the group. This is especially true for therapy and support groups where the members tend to come with different issues or problems they want to discuss or work on.

Example 2

Leader:	Let's begin by going around the room, and you say either "yes" or "no" if there is something you want to bring up in group today. Terry, why don't you start. Yes or no, do you have something you want to talk about?
Terry:	No
Dan:	Yes
Nina:	Yes
Candy:	No
Kim:	No
Lisa:	Yes
Leader:	Those that had yes's, briefly state what your yes is about.

The leader would hear from the three people. Depending on what their issues were, the leader could pick the most pressing one or have them decide whose issue would be brought up first. The main point is that, by using this simple technique, the members get a chance to ask for time during group; and the leader has located the energy in the group.

Following are some other examples of rounds:

On a 1-10 scale, I would like each of you to rate your week. One is you had a terrible week, and 10 is you had a great week.

On a 1-10 scale, I would like each of you to rate how you feel about school. One is you hate it, and 10 is you love it.

In a word or phrase, describe the tone in your house when you were growing up. Some examples may be: war, fun, chaotic, busy, loving, quiet, tense, business.

I'd like to close group today by hearing briefly from each of you as to what stood out to you.

Using a sentence or two, what are you going to think about as a result of being in group today.

As you can see, the rounds give members an opportunity to comment briefly on some topic or issue. The leader and members can then follow-up on the responses by asking questions or asking members to share more about what they meant by their responses.

Focusing on Individuals Within a Group

Whenever counseling is taking place in a group setting, the leader should be the person who is overseeing the counseling (Jacobs et al., 1988; Kotler, 1983). The members may be more active than the leader, but the leader is the person in charge and responsible for what happens. At times, the leader will get other members to comment or share about the issue. At other times, the leader will focus on the "working member" in some specific way.

In the following examples, I describe some possible creative activities that can be utilized when a member is working on a specific issue. In all of the examples, it is assumed that the "working member" has been talking for a few minutes and that the leader has a good grasp of what the person is trying to resolve. There are other ways to approach the different problems, but for the purpose of this book, I present creative approaches that a leader can use. In these examples, I show how the group leader involves members in many different ways when the focus of the group is on an individual. When conducting counseling in a group, I think it is very important that the leader involve the members and not just counsel one member at a time.

Pulling

Often members will talk about being pulled in two directions. By using members, the leader can create this experience physically.

Example 1

The member has been struggling between her desire to pursue a career and her feeling of duty and desire to be home with her children.

Leader: Sally, let's see if acting this out can help you. Sally, I want you, Ted, Carol, and Penny to stand up. *(They all stand.)* Ted, I want you to stand on one side of Sally and pull on one arm, representing her career. You can say back to her the things she has been saying to us here in group. Penny, you are going to take Sally's other arm and represent the mothering aspect in the sense of duty as to what a good mother is. Carol, you are going to play the part of Sally who wants to be home. You pull some on the same arm as Penny. Say the things you have heard her say, but not too loudly because she did not seem too strong on this. Sally, you get in the middle there and all of you pull and talk at the same time. Ready? Go ahead. *(They do this. Ted starts to win, and then Penny pulls hard. A good bit of struggling takes place.)*

Sally: *(Almost crying.)* This is how it feels! I can't take it any more. I wanted so bad for Ted to win.

Sally would probably react to the experience, and then the group would probably continue to focus on Sally for a few minutes in hopes that she would use the experience to help her see what she wants to do.

Example 2

Here, the person has been trying to break free of his parents' control over him.

Leader: Mickey, it is like this. Let me get you to stand up, and I am also going to get Bill and Monica to stand. You are going to be Mickey's mom and dad. *(They all stand.)* Monica, you be Mickey's mom. I want you to stand behind Mickey. *(They move behind him.)* Mickey, in front of you are your goals. I think I'll have the rest of you stand in front of Mickey. *(The three other members stand about 8 feet in front of Mickey.)* You represent his goals, and you are urging him forward by extending your hand out to him and motioning for him to come. Mickey, you are going to try to move to the goals; but as you do, you are going to feel great resistance from your mom and dad, and you will hear all these different things that they say. Everyone have the picture? Bill, Monica, do you know what you are going to do and say? *(They nod.)*

After the struggle, Mickey would probably have a better understanding of what is happening to him, and he more than likely would want to talk about it. Members also may want to share what they experienced being part of the struggle. The experiential activity often proves to be very thought provoking for a number of the members.

Dominating Parent, Spouse, or Boss

Often group members will discuss trouble they are having with someone who seems to dominate them. They feel certain people have some exaggerated power.

In group, Ron has been discussing the problems he has with his wife and mother. He described two recent fights, one with his mother about a cousin's wedding and one with his wife about the way he mows the lawn.

Leader: Ron, let me check something out with the group. What do you hear Ron saying?

Julian: That he's powerless around his wife.

Jan: That he's afraid of his wife just like he was afraid of his mother.

Leader: Let me pick up on what Jan is saying. Jan, I want you and Margo to stand in front Ron, and sort of tower over him. Actually, Jan, I want you to play Ron's mom. So you stand on this chair, while, Margo, you just stand there, representing his wife. *(They position themselves in front of Ron, looming over him.)* Ron, is this how you live?

Ron: *(Meekly, with his eyes down.)* Yes.

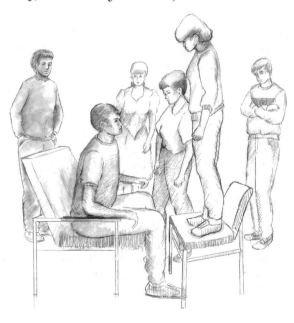

Leader: How does this feel?

Ron: Awful!!

Leader: What do you want to do about it?

The leader has many options at this point depending on Ron's response. She can see if Ron can generate new options for himself. If he can't, she can ask the group for ideas or sharing. Another option would be to have someone else play Ron and have that person rearrange the positions of Jan and Margo so they are not above him and then have the person interact with them as an equal.

Members Playing Other Members

A good technique that allows members to share their insights about a member's work in group is to have the members role-play that member. For instance, in the example above with Ron, the leader could say the following to the members:

Leader: Ron seems to be stuck. I want you to play Ron and express what you think Ron is feeling. Start with, "I'm Ron."

Julian: I'm Ron. I hate this feeling. In fact, I have hated it all my life, but it is familiar. I don't know how else to act.

Margo: I'm Ron. Just once I wish I had the courage to stand up for myself. I am tired of being this way!

Ron: Both of you are so right. Do I really hang my head like the two of you did? *(Everyone nods.)*

Voting

A quick technique that can be very powerful is to have members show their belief in something that the working member is hesitant about. The member will often remember that everyone except him voted a certain way.

Show of Hands Vote

Using the Ron example:

Leader: How many of you believe that Ron can be different? Raise your hands. *(All hands go up except Ron's. Ron sees this and then takes a minute to think.)*

Voice Vote

Leader: Who really is in charge of Ron's life? I am going to ask each of you to say who you think is in charge and who Ron thinks is in charge.

Jan:	Ron is in charge, but he thinks his mom and his wife are.
Shirley:	Ron is in charge. No one else can be.
Margo:	Ron believes someone else is; but Ron, you are in charge–not your wife or mother. It is your life!

Rounds

When a member is talking about some problem, the leader can have the member complete a deepening round which is used to help the member get more into his issue (Jacobs et al., 1988).

Stationary Round

With this technique, the member who is working stays where he is seated.

Leader:	Charles, rather than giving us so much detail and story about moving, I want you to turn to Bill and tell him one thing you are worried about or feeling regarding moving. No story. Look at Bill and say: "One thing I am worried about is," and then complete the sentence.
Charles:	Bill, one thing I am worried about is finding a good house.
Leader:	Now, look at Patti, and start the same way but say something else.
Charles:	Patti, one thing I am worried about is finding good friends.
Leader:	Go to the next person.
Charles:	Joyce, one thing I am worried about is that I can't do the job *(hangs his head down)*.
Leader:	Say that again.
Charles:	*(With a shakey voice)* The thing I am most worried about is that I can't do the job.
Leader:	Say some more about that. I think we are at the real issue now.

Moving Round

There are times when a round can have more effect when the person sits in front of each group member as she speaks.

In this example, the member has been talking about how she feels about herself due to her son's drug problems. She continues to want to tell stories as a way to avoid the pain that she is feeling. The leader decides to use a round to get Molly more in touch with what she is thinking and feeling.

Leader: Molly, do you really want to get a better handle on this? *(She nods yes.)* Good, let's try something different. I want you to take your chair and sit in front of Lucy. Start with: "Because my son has a drug problem" and then finish the sentence. Each of you try to remember what Molly says to you.

Molly: Because my son has a drug problem, uh, *(starts to cry)* I am real scared for him and for me.

Leader: Go to the next person.

Molly: Wayne, because my son has a drug problem I am a failure. *(Cries a little more.)*

Leader: Next person.

Molly: *(Still softly crying)* Because my son has a drug problem, it is wrong for me to be traveling and to be happy.

Leader: Molly, what are you learning from doing this? What stands out to you?

Molly: I don't know.

Leader: *(Speaking in a soft, helpful voice)* Put your chair in the center and listen as the members say back to you what you said to them. *(Speaking to the members)* I want all of you to say aloud, over and over again what Molly said to you. Ready? *(They nod.)* Start...

Molly: *(After listening intently)* No wonder I am in such pain. I have so many fears and negative thoughts running through my head. I think the failure one is the loudest.

Leader: Would you like to spend a few minutes now working on that?

Molly: Yes.

I try to show in the example how powerful this kind of round can be. There are many variations, such as having the person say the same thing as they sit in front of each member. This gives the member a chance to hear his irrational idea over and over again.

Leader: Al, I want you to sit in front of each member and say the sentence you just said. "Because I am not in love with Bonita, I am selfish." Sit in front of each person and say that and experience your feelings and thoughts as you do this.

If the timing and specific sentence is appropriate, the member will usually find this insightful and beneficial. Often he will stop in the middle of the round and say something like, "That's nuts!"

Playing out the Different Ego States

If you use TA in your group counseling, you can have the members role-play a person's different ego states (Corey, 1990). In the example below, the client is trying to decide whether to go home at Christmas time or go on a ski trip. He has been talking about how obligated and guilty he feels, and yet he keeps thinking about how much fun it would be.

Leader: It is obvious that Riley has many different ego states offering opinions about the ski trip. I'd like us to act this out for him. Who can play Riley's Free Child ego state?

Justin: I can.

Leader: Who can play his Guilty Child?

Don: Heck, I can. I do this all the time to myself.

Leader: Who can play the Parent?

Lucinda: I think I can.

Leader: Marcus, I'm going to have you stand in the middle and play Riley's Adult. You do the best you can dealing with all the ego states talking at once.

This is one example of how you can use the members to play the different ego states. There is an unlimited number of creative activities that you can use with TA.

These are just some of the creative techniques that can be used when conducting counseling in a group setting. There are enormous possibilities for using the members in creative ways. Too many group counselors simply conduct individual counseling in a group setting instead of using the members. By your being creative, members most likely will be involved in more ways; and, thus, the group experience will be enhanced for everyone.

8 Creative Marriage and Family Counseling

In this chapter, I discuss the use of creative techniques when conducting marriage and family counseling. The first section covers techniques that can be used when two people in a relationship are both present in the session. The relationship does not have to be a marriage, although most of the examples are of married couples. I also include examples of gay and lesbian couples, since the use of these techniques would basically be the same.

The second section presents ways to use creative counseling with families. I offer numerous examples in hopes of giving you some new and different ways to approach families. In both sections, I use the five kinds of creative techniques that I have discussed throughout this book: props, chairs, movement, writings and drawings, and analogies and fantasies.

Marriage Counseling

Props

Rubber Band

Often couples come to counseling because of the tension between them. A rubber band can be used to demonstrate this tension.

Counselor: This is the second session now; and when I ask if things are any better, you both tell me it is worse. That means you are not understanding the seriousness of this, especially since both of you say you want to stay married. I want to show you what you are doing. Take this rubber band, and each of you pull on it until it is about to snap. *(They both do this and are nervous about the possibility that the rubber band may break.)*
Now, I want you to stretch the band a little bit more. *(They both look at the counselor almost in disbelief.)* That's what you are doing. Instead of lessening the tension this week, you said that it was worse. I can tell you that both of you are going to have to do something different in order to reduce the tension and to allow the two of you to relax. As it is now, there is too much tension!

Wife: That's what I want–the tension to go away.

Husband: This is a great illustration. We have to let up so that the tension goes down.

Blocks

Many marriages can be viewed as trying to put a peg in a hole that is too small. In order to show this to couples, I had a series of blocks made where the peg is much larger than one hole; where the peg nearly fits in one hole; where the peg fits in one hole, and where one hole is much larger than the peg. The progression of hole sizes is to show the various fits of different relationships. Some relationships obviously do not fit; others are close to fitting. Also, the different sizes can show the growth and changes in a relationship. The following examples should give you some ideas of how the blocks may be used.

Example 1: The Bad Fit

Counselor: I want you to look at these blocks. The peg will fit obviously in one, nearly fit in another, and obviously not fit in the third one. What does your marriage look like? Is it a good fit, near fit, or no fit? *(The couple stare at the three blocks and the peg. The wife picks up the blocks and tries each of the fits.)*

Wife: I think it is this impossible fit.

Husband: But we can make it work.

Wife: Only if I give up being what I want to be and shave off some of the peg. It's like you want me to fit your view of a wife. You are the small hole, and I am the peg; and in order to make this work, I have to give up a lot of myself!

Example 2: Growth

Counselor: Here's what seems to be the picture of your marriage. First you started where you, Ken, were ahead of Jane, like the peg is Ken and the small hole is Jane. Later, due to Jane's growth, the two of you experienced a marriage that worked well and fit well. *(The counselor shows them the block and peg that are a good fit.)* Now, Jane, you have grown so much that you feel that there isn't a good fit any more. The hole is you, Jane, and the peg is Ken. *(The counselor demonstrates this by putting the peg in a hole where the peg only fills about half the hole.)*

Jane: That's it! I do feel that I have grown and I need more from Ken. In some ways, I am sorry that I went back to school because I did become so much more aware. But I cannot go back and now, Ken, I need you to grow. That's why we are here for counseling.

Counselor: I think you are at the heart of the matter. Ken, are you willing to try to grow to meet more of Jane's needs? She does want more from you now that she has grown.

Cups

Styrofoam cups can be used in numerous ways to show a couple what may be going on in their marriage.

Example 1

Counselor: Let me show you what I see is going on. Mary, take this cup, which represents your psychological worth. *(Mary holds the cup and stares at it.)* Now, Tod, you take the cup away from Mary and stand on the chair. *(Tod stands on the chair, holding the cup.)* Now, squeeze the cup. *(Mary is looking up and wincing as he does this.)*

Mary: That's how it feels. He smashes me all the time.

Tod: That's because you always screw up!

Counselor: Mary, there are at least two ways not to have your self-worth smashed. Do you know what they are?

Mary: If he'd quit being so critical of me. He acts like my father, not my husband. I don't know what the second one is. Get divorced?

Counselor: That's a temporary solution, but you probably would give your worth to someone else. What about not giving Tod the cup? Why do you put him in charge of your worth?

The counselor would also want to discuss with Tod how he behaves and how he could make some changes. More than likely, the counselor would discuss each of their pasts in terms of their upbringing and previous relationships.

Example 2

Counselor: I want each of you to take a cup. The cup represents your self-esteem. As you go through life, you seek to keep your cup full, so you turn to your partner for re-fueling. Turn to each other and gesture for your partner to pour into your cup. Notice that both of you are so busy trying to get the other to pour into your cup that you don't think to give something to your partner. *(They both nod sheepishly.)*

Miguel: I think I see it now. We try to get from each other rather than give to each other.

Flo: I think we actually try to hurt each other more than we do anything else.

Counselor: Let's do that. Take these pencils and take your partner's cup. Punch holes in your partner's cup.

Flo: That's it! We punch holes in each other's self-esteem. We don't give to each other. How do we stop?

Counselor: That's what we will do in counseling if you both can commit to not trying to hurt the other any more. Do you know how you punch holes in your partner's cup?

Meter

I have used a battery meter that shows if the battery is good, questionable, or bad. The meter is colored and will register green if the battery is charged. I show couples the meter and ask them to comment on what their marriage would register on a meter. I also ask them how they can recharge the marriage. I set the meter on the floor in front of them to remind them of their task, which is to recharge their marriage.

I often refer to the meter during the session when negative interactions are taking place. The purpose is to heightened their awareness of what they do to each other and to have them leave the session with the desire to have their "marriage meter" read positive.

Chairs

In a previous example, the counselor had one of the partners stand on a chair. Another use of chairs is to have the couple move their chairs far apart so that they experience the distance that they have between them. Still another use is to have extra chairs represent other people or things in the couple's life. Often, the chair will represent a parent, but it could represent children, work, or an ex-spouse/lover.

Distance

It is very useful to have movable chairs (as opposed to a couch) when doing relationship counseling. In this example, the counselor has been listening to the couple pick at each other throughout the session, and he realizes that they do not see how much their relationship has deteriorated.

Counselor: I want the two of you to do this. Sit in these two chairs, facing each other. Now move your chairs far apart... That's good. *(The couple's chairs are about 8 feet apart.)* How does this feel?

Diana: In some ways, this feels safer because of the distance; but at the same time, it feels awful because I want to be close to Sam.

Sam: *(In a hostile voice)* If you would talk to me and tell me what is wrong, everything would be okay!! *(Diana spontaneously moves her chair back a little bit.)*

Counselor: Sam, I want you to think about your voice and the way you just said what you did. Diana, why did you move back?

Diana: I want to move away from him when he talks like that.

Counselor: I know, and that is what we have got to stop from happening. We'll talk about the way the two of you interact; but before we do that, I want you to do something for me. I want you to stay in your seats and take each others hands...

Sam: We can't. We are too far apart.

Counselor: Exactly! Somehow we have got to get you close enough to make contact again. The two of you were close at one time, and both of you said that you want your marriage to work. What is it going to take to get you to make contact?

Diana: We both have to move.

Counselor: Not really. One of you could be willing to move way over to meet the other; but from what I am hearing, that is not going to happen, nor should it. I agree that you both need to move. Now think about it *(counselor slows his voice).* What are each of you willing to do to move toward the other so that you can make contact with your partner?

A variation of the chairs being too far apart is to have the couple move the chairs about 5 feet from each other and then ask them to take each other's hands.

Counselor: *(Clients are sitting, facing each other)* I want you to reach out, while staying in your seat, and take your partner's hand.

Joe: What? That's impossible.

Counselor: That's right. Scoot in about a foot and then stretch to reach your partner. *(They do this, but it is obviously a strain to remain in their seats and touch hands.)* How does this feel?

Ann:	Not too much better. It is too much of a stretch. It is uncomfortable.
Counselor:	Good point. I want you both to think for a minute how this applies to your marriage...
Joe:	We have got to get closer, or we will always be reaching. *(Joking to his wife)* Why don't you just pull your chair over here?
Counselor:	I think you both see that each of you will have to give up something. Each needs to move toward the other.

As you can imagine, this can be very powerful if the timing is right. The counselor has many options. He can have the couple return to the couch, or he can conduct the remainder of the session with them sitting far apart. He can also have them move closer or farther apart as the session develops. This helps them to see visually what they are doing to each other.

Chair Representing Person Who Is Not Present

Counselor:	Van, you say that you want to be close to Brenda, but I don't think you see the entire picture. Brenda, you pull your chair next to Van's. How does this feel for both of you?
Brenda:	Good. I wish it could be this way all the time, but it isn't.
Counselor:	I know. Van, how does this feel for you.
Van:	Good. I like this.
Counselor:	Let me show you how it really is. *(The counselor gets two chairs and wedges them between Van and Brenda.)* These chairs represent your ex-wife and your grown daughter. Van, until you finish your business with them, there is always going to be the potential for this wedge.
Brenda:	This is exactly how it feels. At any time, they can call or create some scene; and then Van will either go running to them, become preoccupied with their latest catastrophe, or feel guilty. I hate it!!
Van:	What do you want me to do?
Brenda:	Get some distance between them and us!
Counselor:	That's a good point. In order for there to be no interference, you have to get them farther away than you currently have them. As it now stands, they are right here, ready to wedge between you. What could you do?

Van: *(Thinks for a minute.)* I guess I could move them way across the room.

Counselor: That's true, you could. But will you?

Van: *(Looks at the chairs and then looks at Brenda. Then he picks up the chairs and moves them to the far side of the room.)* I think I see your point. This is where they need to be so that they cannot come between Brenda and me.

Counselor: Very true. Let's work on how to get them in the proper perspective, given that you have been divorced for 3 years and your daughter is 21 years old.

Brenda: I feel better just having the chairs over there. I feel hopeful!

Movement

There are a number of movement activities that the creative counselor can use to help couples experience what they are doing in their relationships.

Out the Door

In the following example, the counselor needs to get the husband to realize how serious the problems are. Tina has told the counselor, in private, that she is ready to leave if things do not change.

Counselor: Leroy, you have been coming for a month now, and Tina says that nothing has changed. What are your thoughts about that?

Leroy: Well, things aren't all that bad, and I feel that my coming here should be proof enough that I care and am going to change.

Tina: No, I want to see some changes in the way you talk to me and the way we spend our weekends and the way you parent our son!!

Leroy: *(Turning to the counselor)* Do you see how upset she gets over nothing?

Counselor: Leroy, I think you need to understand something. Tina, I want you to go to the door and open it and start out of the room. *(Tina does this.)* Good. Stand right there, facing out of the room. Tina, is this close to where you are with the marriage–that is, are you nearly out the door?

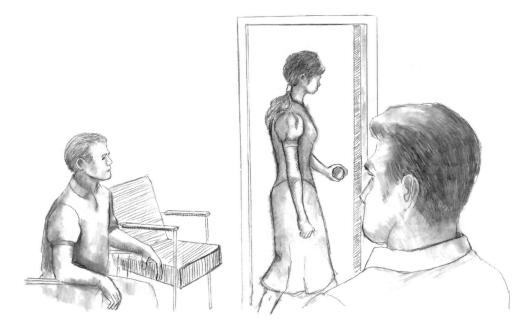

Tina: This is exactly where I am!! *(In a very serious voice)* I don't want a divorce, but I will leave if things don't change. I am really close to saying it is over.

Leroy: *(Staring at Tina in disbelief)* Wait, honey. I had no idea how serious this was. I don't want you to leave. Please come sit down and let's talk.

Something in the Way

Often in relationship counseling, the counselor sees that there is something keeping the couple from relating well with each other. Sometimes a former relationship or a parent will be the obstacle that is interfering. It could also be a job, a hobby, a drug problem, or unfinished business from childhood that is in the way.

In the example below, the counselor has been working with this couple for two sessions on how they can't seem to get very close because Bonnie is holding back. It is apparent to the counselor that Bonnie's attachment to her dad is the source of the problem.

Counselor: It is getting clearer to me as to what I think is going on. Let me get the two of you to stand and face each other. *(They stand about 4 feet apart. The counselor stands between them, looking at Bonnie.)* Bonnie, I want you to hug Tom. Now, I am going to be your father, but you go ahead and hug Tom.

Bonnie: I can't. You are in the way.

Counselor: You can. You just won't be able to do it very well because your father will be in the way. Go ahead and hug Tom. *(Bonnie does this; the counselor is squeezed in the middle. Bonnie finds it hard to make contact with Tom, and she starts to cry.)*

Bonnie: You're so right. I never knew my father had anything to do with my marital problems, but now I see he has everything to do with them. What do I do?

Counselor: I can help you break away from your father and finish the unfinished business that you have with him. Do you want to work on this?

Being Pulled Along Maslow's Hierarchy of Needs

Many couples face the problem of one partner's needs being different from the other's (Maslow, 1968). In the following example, the counselor uses Maslow's hierarchy to show how one person is trying to pull the other forward while the other is trying to pull the first person back.

Counselor: Let me explain something to you that should be of help. A psychologist named Abe Maslow had a theory about our needs and how they are in a hierarchy. I have each of these five needs written on separate sheets of paper, and I am going to place them on the floor about 2 feet apart. I want you to look at them and think where you are in regards to your needs.

The five are: Physiological Needs

Safety and Security Needs

Love and Belonging Needs

Self-esteem Needs

Self-actualizing Needs

Let me briefly explain what each of these are. *(The counselor does this.)* Where do you see yourself?

David: I feel that I am starting to feel real good about myself, and I am wanting to do and try more things. I even think of wanting to move away from the area.

Sue: *(Looking at the counselor)* I just want things to be the way they were. Things were fine. We live next door to my mom and dad which I like a whole lot. He used to like to spend time with them, but now David hardly goes over to see them. He wants me to develop more interests, but I am really afraid to try new things or meet new people.

Counselor: Let's look at the needs on the floor. Where would you be, David, given the way you have been feeling?

David: I think I would put myself with both feet on self-esteem, looking for more.

Sue: I don't know. I guess I would put myself at love and belonging. That's what makes me happy–my family and my husband.

Counselor: I'd like you to stand by the need that you just said. *(They move. David is standing a few feet in front of Sue.)* Now take each other's hand and try to pull your partner to your position. *(They struggle for a bit.)* Okay, stop. Any thoughts?

Sue: That's how it feels. He is always pulling on me and trying to get me to do more. At the same time, I am always nagging him about staying home and going to Mom and Dad's.

David: Why can't you see how dull your life is!!

Counselor: Wait a minute. I don't think it is helpful to attack each other. It is clear to me that the two of you have different needs. The question is what do you do about it? I want you both to see that, because your needs are different, you have some marital stress. But if you are committed to working on this and not pulling at your partner, I think there may be some compromises that can be made that can reduce the fighting and tension. If neither of you is willing to make some compromises, then the problems will continue to exist; and divorce may be the better option.

Writing and Drawing

There are many helpful lists, charts, diagrams, and drawings that can help a couple to see more clearly what is going on and why they have problems.

Marriage–Divorce Assessment

Often during the first session, I try to assess each person's satisfaction level with the relationship and if they want marriage counseling or divorce counseling. Whenever it is not clear to me, I use a variety of assessment techniques or questions.

One technique is to ask them to rate the marriage on a 1-10 scale, with 10 being great and 1 being terrible. I usually write their names on the board and then their rating under it.

Counselor: I want you to see this because it tells me there are some major problems.

	NOW	TWO YEARS AGO
John:	8	9
Liz:	3	7

Often, one partner is relatively happy (8 or 9), and one partner is very unhappy (3 or 4). Seeing this visually sometimes helps the couple, and I can later refer back to their ratings.

Another simple, but useful question to ask is: "Are you here for marriage counseling or divorce counseling?" This gives me some useful information, especially if they disagree. If I want to get this information in visual form, I ask them to mark where they are on the continuum between being married and being divorced and which way the arrow is pointing.

Counselor: On this continuum that I have drawn, where would you put yourself?

Divorced———————————|———————————Married

(Both mark the continuum with an arrow)

Divorced———————————<- |————>———Married

               Emily   Phil

Counselor: Which way is the arrow pointing and why?

Phil: Toward marriage most definitely.

Emily: I'm not sure anymore. The wrong way. Divorce? I am very confused about this marriage and what I want.

The counselor, using this continuum, can make reference to the markings during the session, reminding the couple of what they marked and what they need to do if they want to stay together.

Ratings

Couples in counseling tend to differ in their level of satisfaction about numerous things within a marriage.

Counselor: The two of you seem to be dissatisfied in the way a number of things go in the marriage. You both have complaints about the other. Let's look at your level of satisfaction regarding different aspects of your marriage. I am going to list some of the things you have been talking about; and then I am going to have you each rate how satisfied you are using a 1-10 scale, with 10 being very satisfied. Here are some of the topics that I have heard one or both of you complain about. *(They each provide ratings.)*

	ANN	BOB
Chores	3	9
Time together	2	8
Amount of television	3	10
The way money is spent	4	9
Time spent with friends	3	10
Time with family	9	9
Frequency of sex	7	2
Quality of sex	5	3

Ann: He's happier on some things because he does almost all things to suit himself.

Bob: I want to talk about the sex part!

Counselor: We'll talk about all of them, but first I want us to grasp the big picture. What do each of you see as you look at these ratings?

The counselor can make up the items for the list or have the couple make the list. The important thing is for the couple to see how they rate their satisfaction level on various matters related to their marriage. Listing the ratings can help the counselor when she tries to focus the discussion, and it also makes the couple's differences more concrete.

Priorities

Couples often have very different priorities within the marriage. Listing each person's priorities can prove to be very helpful. Sometimes I let the couple do their own list. Other times, I give them the major categories. The prioritizing of this list by each person can help them to quickly see why they have problems.

Counselor: Does this help the two of you to see why there are problems. Your priorities are quite different.

	HECTOR	ELLEN
Work	1	5
Partner	4	1
Children	5	2
Family of Origin	2	6
Hobbies	6	7
Religion	9	3
Friends	7	4
Sex	3	8
Other	8	9

Hector: My work means everything to me. I have to earn enough for everyone including my parents! She doesn't understand.

Ellen: I knew it! He has me after his family!

Counselor: Wait. The purpose of these ratings is to help you to see why you have problems. I think it is clearer to all three of us what the problems are. Now I hope that counseling can help you to come to some new understandings.

Hector: This chart makes things a lot clearer.

Many times the counselor can spend two or three sessions discussing the priorities, possible compromises, and the problems that are created by their differences.

Egograms

Previously, I discussed the use of an egogram with an individual. Using egograms with couples can be very enlightening as well. The therapist can draw the egograms as she sees the two people, or she can have each partner draw him or herself or the partner (Campos & McCormick, 1972). There are many different ways you can use the egogram. The bar graph helps make clearer why certain interactions continue to occur.

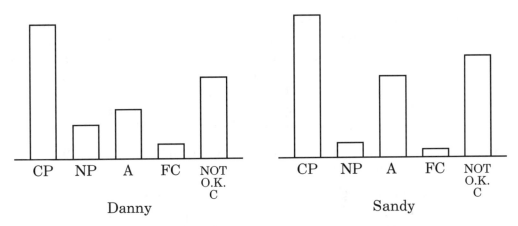

Danny   Sandy

Counselor: What reaction do you have as you look at the two egograms?

Danny: No wonder we don't have much fun. Neither of us have much Free Child.

Sandy: Look at why we fight. Both of our Critical Parents are the largest.

TA Drawings

Earlier, I outlined various ways in which TA can be used to describe interaction patterns with another person. In marriage counseling, I almost always spend some time helping the couple see the way they interact by drawing various interactions, using the TA model of PARENT, ADULT, and CHILD. Clients need a way to understand why things happen, and the TA model is excellent for explaining transactions. I personally believe that marriage counseling can be greatly enhanced by using TA to explain certain interactions. You may want to spend some time exploring this theory if you have not been introduced to it or if you were introduced to it in a way that turned you off. Couples need communication patterns to be made concrete, and TA can help to do this.

Analogies

In Chapter 6, I discussed the use of analogies and how they can be useful for both the client and the counselor. Two of the analogies specifically apply to relationships, so you may want to review those. The "pilot light" analogy can focus couples on whether the relationship can be re-ignited. The "cheerleader" metaphor is excellent for helping partners think through the kind of relationship they have and the kind that they want to have.

Marriage Bank

One analogy that I use frequently with couples deals with the idea of a "marriage bank account."

Counselor: You may want to look at your marriage as an account in a bank. How much do you deposit each day or even each week? Do you only make withdrawals? If that is the case, your account will quickly go to zero. Just like a bank account, you have to make deposits. Deposits in a marriage can be a kiss, a card, a note, or a kind word. Also, it can be warm conversations, sensitivity to the other's feelings, etc.

Jodi: I think we are overdrawn. We haven't made many, if any, deposits lately. Wouldn't you agree?

Ted: You are right, and we said we would never get like this. Heck, lately I feel like all we have been doing is bouncing checks; that is, bouncing each other. I don't want to give up on this marriage. I am willing to make some deposits if you are.

The counselor can use the analogy in many different ways. She can ask each week about the deposits each made. Also, she could have them bring in their "deposit slips," which would be their list of positive things that they have done to enhance the marriage.

As I said in Chapter 6, there are many analogies that can be used. I have given you enough examples to start you thinking about ones that fit your clients. You may even want to get with colleagues and brainstorm about different analogies for the couples you work with.

Fantasies

Having a couple fantasize about their relationship or about some aspect of the relationship can be helpful. Often a couple will use the counseling session to complain and attack their partner, so the use of fantasy may be a way to focus the couple on something productive.

Games

To get couples to take a different look at their relationship, I have asked them to fantasize about what kind of game would describe their relationship.

Example

This is the third session, and the couple has been spending much of the time complaining about the other person.

Rajul: She still has been nagging all week about all kinds of things, and there hasn't been any sex or affection.

Ambuja: You aren't helping out!! You still think I am the cleaning lady!

Counselor: Rather than listening to you cut each other down and complain about the other, let's try something else that I think will be more productive. If you had to describe your relationship in terms of some game that you know, what would that game be and why? By game, I mean any game such as football, boxing, kick boxing, monopoly, chess. Any game that somehow captures, for you, the essence of your relationship.

The value of this fantasy is that it forces the couple to conceptualize their relationship in a different way and it gets them to stop complaining.

Ideal Marriage

Counselor: Rather than focusing on the negative about your partner, I am going to ask each of you to fantasize out loud what an ideal relationship would be. I am going to ask you to fantasize how you would like the daily routine to be, the weekends, vacations, holidays, etc. I will have each of you do this while the other listens and does not interrupt. Think for a minute, and then I will have one of you go first... Who wants to start?

Bobbi: I will.

Counselor: Good. I want you to close your eyes and imagine your ideal relationship. How would the morning be?...

There are many variations to this, depending on what the counselor is trying to get the couple to discuss. Having one person listen to her partner's dreams can be a very powerful, moving experience that can lead to some in-depth counseling.

Family Counseling

Many of the creative techniques described throughout this book may prove to be useful in working with families. This section presents a few specific techniques that you may want to use with families that you are seeing.

Moving the Chairs

In families there are various sub-groups, or one person is obviously being put in the middle of the parents, or one person may feel isolated (Bowen, 1978; Minuchin & Fishman, 1981). Having people move their chairs to show the interaction patterns in the family can help make the family dynamics more concrete.

Counselor: *(To Amy, who is 13 years old)* I want you to take your chair and move it way to the other side of the room and sit there. Ruth, you and Bill move together. *(Everyone does this, and the counselor moves her chair to be about equidistant between the couple and their daughter.)* How does this feel?

Amy: How it is! They don't understand me—we are miles apart on everything!

Ruth: I want to be close to Amy, but I can't stand the way she acts. She does no school work, and she hangs out with losers!

Counselor: How does the distance feel?

Bill: Something is wrong with our family, and I hope you can fix us. I do not want this distance. In fact, sometimes I feel in the middle.

Counselor: That's a good point. Why don't you move your chair into the middle.

Amy: This is an accurate picture. Dad's not on me as much, but he has to side with Mom.

As you can see, there are many different ways to use the movement of the chairs and the people. Frequently when a teenager is isolated, I move my chair next to him or her so the teen feels supported by someone. This also helps to prevent the feeling of being "ganged-up on" by the adults.

Using an Empty Chair

Many times during family counseling, all involved people are not at the session. Often there is a divorced parent, a disliked boyfriend, a stepparent, or some other person who is significant to the family dynamics who is not in attendance. The use of an empty chair to represent that person can make the picture clearer to everyone.

Counselor: Carol, you are saying that if Mom did not have this boyfriend, things would be much better. I want you and your mom to move your chairs away from each other, and I am going to put this chair between you. The chair represents Mom's boyfriend. Is this how you see it–is he between you?

Carol: That's how it is. Mom spends all her time with him and ignores me.

Mom: Carol, I am lonely, and he is nice to me. I like being with him, and you are nearly 14. You don't need me.

Counselor: *(In a kind, but firm voice)* Wait a minute. You honestly don't believe she needs you?

Mom: Well, I thought she didn't. Not like when she was 6.

Counselor: It is different than when she was 6, but she does need you. Do you hear her and see the wedge that is between you? *(Mom looks at the chair. They both begin to cry.)*

By using the empty chair to bring various people into the session, the counseling is made clearer for everyone. It also gives the counselor something to refer to when discussing the absent person.

Standing on the Chair

If one of the family members is a dominating force within the family and is present in the session, I often have that person stand on a chair. This could be the alcoholic, the rageaholic, or the super critical person. This could also be an illness or handicap of some sort. When everyone experiences this image, valuable discussion usually takes place, and some movement in the therapy process will occur. The timing of this activity is crucial. If it is tried too early in therapy, it may anger the person on the chair.

Counselor: This is our third session, and I believe I am getting the picture of what is going on in the family. In order for this family to get better, some things have to change. One of them is the role that Dad plays in the family. Dad, I am going to ask you to stand on this chair in the center of the family, because I think this is how you try to be with your family. *(Dad stands on the chair.)*

Connie: That's it. He thinks he's the almighty or something! I'm only 12, but I'm not going to treat him like a god.

Gerry: I think he wants us to feel small around him, but I don't anymore. He drinks, smokes, and says stupid things all the time.

Mom: *(To the counselor)* Do you see what I mean? There is this constant battle for power, and I am protecting everyone. I'm tired.

Counselor: The key for the family is to figure out some new ways of interacting. Dad, what do you think of all this?

Dad: Obviously, trying to be up here is not working. Boy, it sure did for my dad though! I don't know how else to do it.

Counselor: That's why we are here–to learn new and better ways to communicate. Come down off the chair.

Connie: Oh, I wish it could be this way.

Sculpt How You Feel Being in the Family

This example is a variation of the one above in that the entire family positions themselves as to how they feel in the family.

Counselor: I think it may be helpful for everyone in the family to see how everyone else is feeling about being in the family. What I want you to do is stand and make a circle... Now, in a minute I am going to ask you to sculpt yourself as to how you feel about this family, using your entire body. Let me explain. If you feel very open and safe and into the family, you would move to the center and leave your arms down, indicating you are open. If, on the other hand, you feel afraid and out of the family, you would put your hands up around your face indicating fear, and turn your back to the family. Use your arms and body position to indicate how you feel. Any questions?... Ready, everyone take a position.

Once the family members take a position, the family counselor has numerous options. He can have each person comment on her position or on the family as a whole. He can talk about changes or how it feels looking at the "sculpture." This proves to be very valuable for both the family and the therapist.

A variation of sculpturing is called "family sculpture" which has been written about in many family therapy textbooks (Fenell & Weinhold, 1989; Nichols & Schwartz, 1991). Family sculpture is similar to what I described above except one family member at a time would arrange the members of his family into a family sculpture as seen through his eyes. This usually proves to be a powerful, therapeutic activity.

Distance

Counselor: There is much emotional distance in your family. Most of you are just isolated with very little connection to each other. I want you to stand and make a large circle with a lot of space between you. *(They all do this.)* Is this how it feels?

Sam: I don't feel connected to anyone.

Counselor: JoAnn, trade places with Cammy, but keep plenty of space between you and Sam.

Cammy: We all just exist in the house together.

Eddie: I sometimes wish I lived in a different family.

Counselor: Let me do something that may feel better for you, Eddie, and for everyone. I'd like you to move in closer and make a circle, holding hands. How does this feel?

JoAnn: *(With tears in her eyes)* Better. I want it to be this way.

Eddie: I am happy to see Mom and Dad holding each other's hand.

As you can see, several different reactions and emotions can come out of performing this activity. You can keep the family holding hands or have them go back to the way they were and talk about what it is going to take to get to the "hand holding" position.

Ratings

Listing each family member's rating of various aspects of family living can help the family to see how everyone feels about certain issues. I usually use a 1-10 rating on such issues as fun in the family, feeling of trust, or liking to be in the family. By having everyone give the issue a rating, family members can see where they need to improve. This often is very valuable for parents because it makes things concrete.

Counselor: What do you see as you look at the ratings? This is how you rated life in your family. Remember 10s would be the highest.

	MOM	DAD	LESLIE	ALEX
Fun	2	6	3	6
Supportive	1	7	5	8
Cooperation	1	5	3	3
Marital Relationship	3	7	3	4
Sibling Relationship	2	2	2	2

Dad: Things are bad, and Mom seems to feel the worst. I didn't realize how people were feeling. Also, we need to work on our marriage, and the kids need to get some things straightened out.

Leslie: I want us to be happy. I can do better with Alex, and I'll try to be more cooperative.

Mom: I feel better getting all this out so that everyone can see the problems. I always felt like we needed to work together, and this is a start.

Tone in the Home

A quick exercise to use with families is to have each member think of a word or phrase that describes his home life as he sees it. I usually do this during the first or second session, because it serves as a way to assess how each person feels about living in the family.

Counselor: I'd like to ask you to each think about the tone in your home, and then I am going to have you share what you come up with. By tone, I mean the atmosphere or the underlying theme. Here are some examples: comfortable, war, business, caring, chaotic, supportive, fighting. Get the idea?... Everyone have something?

Mom: Hurried and cautious.

Dad: Lazy. I feel like I have to ride herd over everyone.

Toni: Uncomfortable. Do, do, do!!!

Mick: Confusing.

Counselor: Let's take a look at what you said and what you would like to see as the tone. The tone in a home is very important, and I feel that we could work in these sessions to create a different tone for your family. What do you think?

These are just a few of the creative techniques that could be used when conducting marriage and family counseling. Actually a whole book on creative counseling could be written for just marriage and family counselors.

References

Axline, V. (1969). *Play therapy* (rev. ed.). New York: Ballantine.

Berne, E. (1972). *What do you say after you say hello?* New York: Bantam Books.

Bowen, M. (1978). *Family therapy in clinical practice.* New York: Jason Aronson.

Bradshaw, J. (1988). *Bradshaw on: The family.* Deerfield, FL: Health Communications, Inc.

Branden, N. (1987). *How to raise your self-esteem.* New York: Bantam Books.

Campos, L. P. (1988). *You can redecide your life.* Sacramento: Sacramento Institute for Redecision Therapy.

Campos, L., & McCormick, P. (1972). *Introduce your marriage to transactional analysis.* Sacramento: Sacramento Institute for Redecision Therapy.

Campos, L., & McCormick, P. (1985). *Introduce yourself to transactional analysis.* Sacramento: Sacramento Institute for Redecision Therapy.

Carter, S. R. (1987). Use of puppets to treat traumatic grief: A case study. *Elementary School Guidance and Counseling, 21,* 210-215.

Carkhuff, R. R. (1987). *The art of helping* (6th ed.). Amherst, MA: Human Resource Development Press.

Cavanagh, M. E. (1990). *The counseling experience* (reissue). Prospect Heights, IL: Wavelan.

Corey, G. (1990). *Theory and practice of group counseling.* Pacific Grove, CA: Brooks/Cole.

Corey, G. (1991). *Theory and practice of counseling and psychotherapy.* Pacific Grove, CA: Brooks/Cole.

Corey, G., Corey, M., Callanan, P., & Russel, J. M. (1988). *Group techniques.* Pacific Grove, CA: Brooks/Cole.

Cormier, W. H., & Cormier, L. S. (1985). *Interviewing strategies for helpers: Fundamental skills and cognitive behavioral interventions* (2nd ed.). Pacific Grove, CA: Brooks/Cole.

Corsini, R. J., & Wedding, D. (1989). *Current psychotherapies* (4th ed.). Itasca, IL: F. E. Peaccock.

Dinkmeyer, D. C., Dinkmeyer, D. C., Jr., & Sperry, L. (1987). *Adlerian counseling and psychotherapy* (2nd ed.). Columbus, OH: Charles E. Merrill.

Dreikurs, R. (1953). *Fundamentals of Adlerian psychology.* Chicago: Alfred Adler Institute.

Dusay, J. (1980). *Egograms*. New York: Bantam.

Egan, G. (1990). *The skilled helper* (4th ed.). Pacific Grove, CA: Brooks/Cole.

Ellis, A. (1962). *Reason and emotion in psychotherapy*. New York: Lyle Stuart.

Ellis, A., & Dryden, W. (1987). *The practice of rational-emotive therapy*. Secaucus, NJ: Lyle Stuart.

Ellis, A., & Harper, R. (1975). *A new guide to rational living*. Englewood Cliffs, NJ: Prentice-Hall.

Feder, E., & Feder, B. (1981). *The expressive arts therapies: Art, music, and dance as psychotherapy*. Englewood Cliffs, NJ: Prentice-Hall.

Fenell, D. L., & Weinhold, B. K. (1989). *Counseling families*. Denver: Love.

Forward, S. (1986). *Men who hate women & the women who love them*. New York: Bantam Books.

Freud, S. (1955). *The interpretation of dreams*. London: Hogarth Press.

Gilliland, B. E., & James, R. K. (1988). Crisis intervention strategies. Pacific Grove, CA: Brooks/Cole.

Gladding, S. T. (1991). *Group work*. New York: Merrill.

Gladding, S. T. (1992). *Counseling as an art: The creative arts in counseling*. Alexandria, VA: American Association for Counseling and Development.

Haley, J. (1986). *Uncommon therapy*. New York: W. W. Norton.

Halpern, H. M. (1982). *How to break your addiction to a person*. New York: Bantam Books.

Hill, L. (1992). *Fairy tales: Visions for problem resolution in eating disorders*. Journal of Counseling and Development, 70, 584-588.

Jacobs, E. E., Harvill, R. L., & Masson, R. L. (1988). *Group counseling: Strategies and skills*. Pacific Grove, CA: Brooks/Cole.

James, M., & Jongeward, D. (1978). *Born to win: transactional analysis with Gestalt experiments*. New York: Signet.

James, R. K., & Myer, R. (1987). Puppet: The elementary school counselor's right or left arm. *Elementary School Guidance and Counseling, 21*, 292-299.

Kottler, J. A. (1983). *Pragmatic group leadership*. Pacific Grove, CA: Brooks/Cole.

Landreth, G. L. (1991). *Play therapy: The art of the relationship*. Muncie, IN: Accelerated Development.

Levy, F. (1988). *Dance movement therapy*. Reston, VA: National Dance Association.

Love, P. (1990). *The emotional incest syndrome.* New York: Bantam Books.

Maslow, A. (1968). *Toward a psychology of being* (rev. ed.). New York: Van Nostrand Reinhold.

McKinney, F. (1976). Free writing as therapy. *Psychotherapy: Theory Research and Practice, 13,* 183-187.

Meier, S. T. (1989). *The elements of counseling.* Pacific Grove, CA: Brooks/Cole.

Mellody, P. (1989). *Facing codependence.* San Francisco: Harper & Row.

Mintz, E. E. (1982). On the rationale of touch in psychotherapy. In R. M. Suinn & R. G. Weigel (Eds.), *The innovative psychological therapies: critical and creative contributions.* New York: Harper & Row.

Minuchin, S., & Fishman, H. C. (1981). *Family therapy techniques.* Cambridge, MA: Harvard University Press.

Nichols, M. P., & Schwartz, R. C. (1991). *Family therapy concepts and methods.* Boston: Allyn and Bacon.

Nicholson, J. A., & Golsan, G. (1983). *The creative counselor.* New York: McGraw-Hill.

Nickerson, T., & O'Laughlin, K. (1982). *Helping through action/action-oriented therapies.* Amherst, MA: Human Resource Development Press.

Norwood, R. (1985). *Women who love too much.* Los Angeles: Jeremy P. Tarcher.

Nugent, F. A. (1990). *An introduction to the profession of counseling.* Columbus: Merrill Publishing Company.

Okun, B. F. (1992). *Effective helping.* Pacific Grove, CA; Brooks/Cole.

Passons, W. R. (1975). *Gestalt approaches in counseling.* New York: Holt, Rinehart, & Winston.

Perls, F. (1969). *Gestalt therapy verbatim.* Moab, UT: Real People Press.

Perls, F. (1973). *The Gestalt approach and eye witness to therapy.* New York: Bantam Books.

Polster, E., & Polster, M. (1973). *Gestalt therapy integrated.* New York: Brunner/Mazel.

Progoff, I. (1975). *At a journal workshop.* New York: Dialogue House.

Riley, S. (1987). *The advantages of art therapy in an outpatient clinic.* American Journal of Art Therapy, 26, 21-29.

Rogers, C. (1951). *Client-centered therapy.* Boston: Houghton Mifflin.

Rogers, R. L., & McMillin, C. S. (1989). *Don't help: A positive guide to working with the alcoholic.* New York: Bantam.

Shulman, L. (1984). *The skills of helping* (2nd ed.). Itasca, IL: F. E. Peacock Publishers.

Steiner, C. (1974). *Scripts people live: Transactional analysis of life scripts.* New York: Grove Press.

Stevens, J. O. (1971). *Awareness.* Lafayette, CA: Real People Press.

Stewart, I., & Joines, V. (1987). *TA today.* Chapel Hill, NC: Lifespace Publishing.

Trotzer, J. P. (1989). *The counselor and the group.* Muncie, IN: Accelerated Development.

Wadeson, H. (1987). *The dynamics of art psychotherapy.* New York: John Wiley & Sons.

Walen, S. R., DiGiuseppe, R., & Wessler, R. L. (1980). *A practitioner's guide to rational-emotive therapy.* New York: Oxford.

Willison, B., & Masson, B. (1986). *The role of touch in therapy: An adjunct to communication.* Journal of Counseling and Development, 64, 497-500.

Wubbolding, R. E. (1986). *Using reality therapy.* New York: Harper & Row.

Young, M. E. (1992). *Counseling methods and techniques: An eclectic approach.* New York: Merrill.

Zinker, J. (1977). *Creative process in Gestalt therapy.* New York: Vintage Books.